A Taste of Grace

A
Taste
of
Grace

Christianity Without the Religion

By Greg Albrecht

Published by Plain Truth Ministries, Pasadena, CA

Unless otherwise indicated, all Scripture passages are from the Holy Bible, New International Version (NIV) copyright ©1973, 1978, 1984, 2011 by International Bible Society.
Used by permission of Zondervan Publishing House.
All rights reserved.

Library of Congress Cataloging-in-Publication Data

Albrecht, Greg. 1947 -
A Taste of Grace /
Greg Albrecht

p. cm.
Includes biographical references and index.

Cover photo by Design Pics; Caley Tse
ISBN-978-1-889973-11-1

1. Theology, Doctrinal—Popular works.
2. Christianity—Miscellanea
I. Title

CONTENTS

ACKNOWLEDGEMENTS   6
FOREWORD   8

Chapter One
EVERYONE IS WELCOME (*Matthew 22:1-14*)   17

Chapter Two
THE GREAT REVERSAL (*Matthew 20:1-16*)   32

Chapter Three
"ALL IS FORGIVEN, LOVE PAPA" (*Matthew 18:21-*35)   45

Chapter Four
A TALE OF TWO NOBODIES (*Luke 10:25-37*)   58

Chapter Five
HE BECOMES ONE OF THE FLOCK (*John 10:1-18*)   71

Chapter Six
UNCIRCULATED, MINT CONDITION GRACE?
(*Matthew 25:14-30*)   89

Chapter Seven
THE SHREWD OPERATOR (*Luke 16:1-15*)   102

Chapter Eight
A FIELD TRIP TO A "HOLY" PLACE (*Mark 12:35-44*)   113

Chapter Nine
THE MEMBER AND THE NON-MEMBER
(*Luke 18:9-14*)   124

Chapter Ten
A FATHER'S UNRESERVED & UNDESERVED LOVE
(*Luke 15:1-32*)   136

AFTERWORD: TWO CAPTAINS   156

Acknowledgements:

Books are not the sole production of the author whose name appears on the cover—they are created and generated by a team. My motivation and inspiration for *A Taste of Grace* comes from standing on the shoulders of thousands of men and women around the world, and the personal stories they have shared with me. Each one of them is, as I am, a survivor of a perilous religious journey.

Because I have experienced the miracle of God's grace, I am passionate about its power, which enables religious refugees to rise in Christ, phoenix-like, out of the ashes.

May these pages prove to be good news for those who are now trying to make sense of God, for those who are currently incarcerated in a spiritual prison, as well as for those who are experiencing the aftermath of a traumatic experience inflicted on them by a religious institution. The joy of God's grace more than compensates for the bondage endured at the hands of performance-based religion.

Many individuals had some part in the production of this manuscript. I wish to express my deepest appreciation to Laura Urista and Marv Wegner, co-workers at Plain Truth Ministries, for their expertise and contributions. I thank Bert Gary and Brad Jersak, for their advice and suggestions, helping to improve the final product.

As with all of my books, and for that matter the last 42 years of my life, my wife Karen has been a sounding board, as well as providing support and proofreading and commentary. Her most recent battle with cancer has only served to deepen my love. Karen—you are forever my *Unchained Melody*.

I have studied the teachings and parables of Jesus for many years, and while God's grace has been by far and away the most vital part of my insights, the writings and examples of many fellow Christ-followers have helped me along the way. Samuel Johnson once said that in order to write one book a writer must read "half a library."

Without attempting to rank their influence, or to pretend I understand all of their considerable insights, I am thankful to Martin Luther, Joachim Jeremias, Dietrich Bonhoeffer, Jacques Ellul, Lewis Smedes, Soren Kierkegaard, Frederick Buechner, Fyodor Dostoevsky, Jim Fowler, C.S. Lewis, N.T. Wright, Robert Farrar Capon and Brennan Manning for influencing my thoughts about Jesus and God's amazing grace.

When I was in the second grade, my mother attempted (with little success) to attract some of my attention away from playing baseball to playing the piano. During my years of enforced piano lessons I became aware of (and later in awe of) the musical genius of Johann Sebastian Bach—often known simply as JSB.

After my baseball and piano playing days were over, I learned of a superscript/subscript Bach placed on almost all of his compositions "—SDG" (*Soli Deo Gloria*)—Latin for "to God alone be the glory." While my attempts to play the piano always fell far short of doing justice to the compositions of JSB, I am humbled to join him, thanking God for his mercy and grace which enable me to share *A Taste of Grace*.

—SDG

FOREWORD

Grace for Exploited and Abused Nobodies

Take a good look, friends, at who you were when you got called into this life. I don't see many of the "brightest and the best" among you, not many influential, not many from high-society families. Isn't it obvious that God deliberately chose men and women that the culture overlooks and exploits and abuses, chose these "nobodies" to expose the hollow pretensions of the "somebodies"? That makes it quite clear that none of you can get by with blowing your own horn before God. Everything that we have—right thinking and right living, a clean slate and a fresh start—comes from God by way of Jesus Christ. That's why we have the saying, "If you are going to blow a horn, blow a trumpet for God." —1 Corinthians 1:26-31, The Message

Biblical word pictures of streams and rivers illustrate the free-flowing grace of God, and by contrast, deserts and parched places portray empty souls cut off from God. Those who find themselves wandering far from the river of life wither, and become spiritually dehydrated.

God's grace flows downward, from divinity to humanity. It's like water in that it flows to low places, responding favorably to the spiritual gravitational pull of humility. God's grace is normally resisted by religious high places—but welcomed in the lowest of places.

God gives his grace to those who have been humbled, while he resists the spiritually proud (1 Peter 5:5). God's grace is experienced by many who are well aware of their spiritual needs, and therefore willingly come to the river of life. By contrast, those who believe themselves to be spiritually sufficient see no need to make their spiritual home by the banks of the river of life. The spiritually proud see God's grace as unnecessary—it cascades off their souls like the proverbial "water off a duck's back." God's grace thrives in the lives of nobodies who have been overlooked, exploited, abused and abandoned. When we are down and out we find it far easier to be convinced we are in desperate need of God's grace.

When Alcoholics Anonymous (AA) was first beginning, two opposing groups divided about how they would best help alcoholics. One group, which was called the Oxford Group, required its members to commit to a Christian creed. The Oxford Group essentially believed that its members could work themselves out of alcoholism.

The other group insisted on grace as its foundation—this group, which became the AA we know today—insisted that the only way that alcoholics could deal with their addictions was through grace. They decided not to hide the past, but rather, at the beginning of each AA meeting, each person was encouraged to say, "Hi, I'm…and I'm an alcoholic."

This practice in AA, which continues to this day, is not a white flag signaling capitulation to addiction, but rather surrender to a "higher power" who must deliver and redeem a person from alcoholism. AA speaks of God as a "higher power" for its goal is to help people of all faiths and for those who have no faith. A higher power must do for addicts that which addicts cannot do for themselves. Like water, God's grace flows to low places. Grace involves dependence on the part of the addict—not independence. Accepting God's grace involves surrender, and few things are as hard to surrender as cherished religious ceremonies, observances and icons.

God's grace is at the heart of the relationship God offers to you and me—it's the foundation of that relationship. God's grace, in turn, flows out of God's love—and God's love is the very essence and nature of who he is. But we must understand that God's generous offer of grace is on his terms, not on ours. His terms are that we surrender all Christless traditions and conventions that attempt to persuade us that in some way our efforts, through our religious exercises, rituals and performances will enable us to grow more righteous, develop more holiness or build more character—making us spiritually sufficient apart from him.

When we do something that we have been assured makes God more pleased with us than he would have been had we not done so, pride is the inevitable result. Some even propose that God is obligated to respond to our religious deeds. The whole performance-based culture leads to spiritual arrogance—with many pridefully concluding:

"I'm-better-than-others because of all the special and unique things I do."

God opposes religious pride and arrogance while giving grace to the humble. God's grace is a summary statement of Jesus' ministry. Jesus consistently opposed the high and mighty, haughty and arrogant, spiritually entitled religious institutionalism of his day, and instead preferred simple fishermen, lepers, prostitutes, lowly tax collectors, despised shepherds, and yes—even women, who were regarded as second-class citizens.

Jesus was grace personified.

Sadly, within Christ-less religion, which predominates in Christendom today, grace is only a word. Why is it that so much of Christendom, ostensibly composed of Christ-followers, is filled with hatred, rage, competition, arrogance and arguments about doctrine, beliefs and creeds? The New Testament overflows with God's grace. Whatever happened to his grace?

Within Christ-less religion the emphasis is on what individuals can do to make themselves more pleasing to God. Within authentic Christianity, individuals must surrender the idea that they can take care of their own spiritual problems. Accepting grace, which comes from God by way of Jesus Christ, involves an acceptance of the supremacy of the Master, our Lord and Savior Jesus Christ.

Opening Our Hands and Hearts

Augustine, one of the early church fathers, once said that God wants to give us good things but our hands are too full to receive them. God always reaches out to us with his grace, but in order to receive his grace we must be willing to empty our hands and hearts of the religion that we hold near and dear.

If we release the performance-based way of relating to God and open our hands and hearts to him, God will fill us with the riches of his grace. God's grace is the currency—the medium of exchange—of the kingdom of heaven. God freely gives us all the spiritual resources we will ever need, if we will only agree to accept his grace. All that we ever need in order to know and experience God has been accomplished for us, in and through the work of Jesus Christ. It's D-O-N-E.

By contrast, the currency of the kingdom of religion is D-O. The kingdom of religion relentlessly screams at us: "Show me your spiritual money! Earn your own way. Demonstrate what you are doing for the kingdom of religion. Prove yourself. Work harder. Do more. Your account is overdrawn. Put in some overtime. Light more candles, say more prayers, attend church more often—get with the program!"

God's kingdom of heaven operates on an entirely different spiritual platform than the kingdoms of our world. Religious deeds and accomplishments are worthless in the kingdom of heaven—they are like counterfeit or Monopoly money. Currency we earn by our hard work and efforts has no value in the kingdom of heaven.

We have nothing to offer God that he doesn't already have. We can't buy or purchase God's favor. Without God's grace, the hardest working saint you know is spiritually impoverished. The most righteous person you can ever hope to meet, apart from the righteousness which comes only from God, will never accrue spiritual treasures they can use in the kingdom of heaven. God gives his grace to those who recognize their need, and are willing to sell all that they value and cherish. God gives his grace to those who surrender all their spiritual treasures and trophies, and come and follow Jesus.

The kingdom of heaven is all about God's goodness, holiness and righteousness, which he offers to us, by his grace. If we accept the invitation of his love and grace, then we do so without any strings attached. We cannot import religious artifacts and customs into the kingdom of heaven. God is opposed to legalistic religion with all its Christ-less religious rituals, ceremonies and performances because it drives us away from him. The kingdom of religion makes us proud of what we do and what we accomplish—it deludes and deceives us.

The kingdom of religion encourages many to labor under the false premise that God is trying to fix them. Thus, they perceive their relationship with God as a spiritual behavior modification program. But God is not simply trying to fix and repair us. He is not at all interested in applying religious super-glue to our souls. God is interested in our complete transformation. He offers us, by his grace, a new life in Christ—a spiritual reality we cannot earn.

Resting in Christ

The announcement of the kingdom Jesus proclaimed was and is incredibly great news! The gospel of Jesus Christ is a revolutionary declaration that the old is gone, and the new has come (see 2 Corinthians 5:17 and Revelation 21:4-5). Through his birth, life, death and resurrection Jesus brought a new spiritual kingdom to this earth. It's often been said that Jesus didn't come to start another religion—he offered salvation from the havoc wreaked by the kingdom of religion. Neither did Jesus come to offer cosmetic reforms to the kingdom of religion. He came with new wine, a new covenant and a new way of relating to God. He didn't come to add to the problem of our shame and guilt—he came to introduce and offer the solution!

In the beginning, when God finished his work of creation he rested. He obviously wasn't tired—he didn't need time to catch his breath. He rested in the sense that the work was over—nothing more needed to be done to the physical creation. *His work was finished.* In the old covenant the seventh-day Sabbath was a memorial of creation, and in this physical covenant the emphasis was on physical performance and deeds. Thus, under the old covenant, the people of God didn't physically work on the seventh day. Physical rest was the physical footing laid down by the old covenant Sabbath, but it was only a shadow (Colossians 2:17) of the Messianic reality of spiritual rest.

However, religion overshadowed and obscured any deeper significance of Sabbath rest, so that the seventh-day day itself, rather than its divine Reality, became just another obligation. The seventh day, along with the other rules and restrictions of the old covenant, became a religious ritual, devoid of any spiritual significance. The Sabbath came to be virtually idolized as the sign of those who were God's people, compared to those who were not. The Sabbath, along with other old covenant stipulations, was enthroned by the religion of Jesus' day as a central part of its distinctive, esoteric and exclusive identity. Religion assured its followers that they were God's people because they observed the Sabbath. Law keeping and law breaking became, in their eyes, the criteria of one's relationship with God.

The Sabbath was one of the major controversies of Jesus' ministry and teachings. Time and time again Jesus clashed with Sabbath-religion. Astonished Sabbath-keepers heard him declare himself as Lord of the Sabbath (Mark 2:28). The gospel of Jesus Christ first diminished and then devalued the past identity of the first Christians (all of whom were, originally, Jewish Sabbath-keepers) and within a few decades demolished it. The physical Sabbath was obsolete, because the gospel of Jesus Christ insisted that relationship with God was based on identity with Jesus, not the Sabbath.

Jesus identified himself as *I AM*, a title or name for God that came to be seen by that law-obsessed community as so sacred that it could not even be spoken. Jesus, God the Son, was the Creator who had rested on the seventh day to begin with—he finished that work. And now he had come to earth to finish another work. He came to finish off performance-based religion and give all humanity true rest. He came to announce another way to know and be known by God. He came to fulfill all of the requirements of the old covenant. When he finished his mission, effectively ending religion as a method by which humanity might experience God, he said, *"It is finished"* (John 19:30).

Rest in Christ turned religious conjectures and suppositions about *how God should work* right-side up. Christ-less religion then, during Jesus' earthly ministry, and ever since that time, believes that

God should reward the faithful, hardworking and obedient. According to religion, one prerequisite for receiving God's favor is physically resting on a pre-scribed day. In addition to a long and formidable list of stipulations, Christ-less religion believes that God should work through its own conventional religious institutions and structures—through its trained and educated clergy—certainly not through some untrained and unlettered carpenter.

But it was the Carpenter from Nazareth who came to reveal God. Jesus of Nazareth did not con-form to the structures and methodologies of religion. His unconventional teaching proclaimed grace, offering true rest, including much-needed rest from performance-based religion as the way to relate to God.

It is with rest in Christ in mind that I invite you to catch a glimpse of grace in the teachings of Jesus. *A Taste of Grace* offers appetizing samples of God's grace through Jesus' parables and stories and metaphors and analogies—as well as in his straight from the shoulder no-holds-barred confrontations with religion and its leadership. By God's grace, the pages that follow offer a taste of the unvar-nished, original and authentic grace evident in selected teachings of Jesus.

The kingdom of religion is all about paying your dues and making your own way. It's all about earn-ing and getting what you deserve. *Christianity Without the Religion* is all about God's unmerited favor—it's called grace!

CHAPTER 1

EVERYONE IS WELCOME

Jesus spoke to them again in parables, saying: "The kingdom of heaven is like a king who prepared a wedding banquet for his son. He sent his servants to those who had been invited to the banquet to tell them to come, but they refused to come.

Then he sent some more servants and said, 'Tell those who have been invited that I have prepared my dinner: My oxen and fattened cattle have been butchered, and everything is ready. Come to the wedding banquet.'

But they paid no attention and went off—one to his field, another to his business. The rest seized his servants, mistreated them and killed them. The king was enraged. He sent his army and destroyed those murderers and burned their city.

Then he said to his servants, 'The wedding banquet is ready, but those I invited did not deserve to come. So go to the street corners and invite to the banquet anyone you find.' So the servants went out into the streets and gathered all the people they could find, the bad as well as the good, and the wedding hall was filled with guests.

But when the king came in to see the guests, he noticed a man there who was not wearing wedding clothes. He asked, 'How did you get in here without wedding clothes, friend?' The man was speechless.

Then the king told the attendants, 'Tie him hand and foot, and throw him outside, into the darkness, where there will be weeping and gnashing of teeth.'

For many are invited, but few are chosen."
—Matthew 22:1-14

Babette's Feast, a short story and film, revolves around two unmarried sisters who live in an isolated village in Denmark. Forsaking husbands and children, they dedicate their lives to helping their father, the pastor of a small church he founded. They determine to remain true to their father's proclamation of salvation through rigorous self-denial. The story centers on their lives in the latter years of the 19th century as they attempt to faithfully follow the repressive practices of their father, even after his death. Along with a small group of followers the sisters are devoted to keeping his legalistic teachings alive in the village. But as the years pass the sisters find it difficult to preside over the people they shepherd, as disagreements and bickering among them grows, centered on specific religious traditions and customs around which their individual lives have been shaped.

Babette is a refugee who arrives in the village having fled a civil war in France. She goes to work as a maid and cook for the two spinsters and in the process becomes very much aware of how the performance-based religion to which the sisters are devoted spiritually paralyzes them and those they lead. Babette has worked for them 14 years when the sisters decide to attempt to unite the little group dedicated to their father's teachings by holding a celebration on what would have been his 100th birthday.

Just as the sisters start to plan a simple and plain birthday celebration (anything more would have been scandalous in terms of their father's spiritual legacy), Babette learns that she has just won a French lottery. It seems that an old friend had entered her name in the lottery every year—and Babette discovers she has the winning ticket.

Babette offers to share her good fortune by creating a sumptuous feast, preparing and serving French gourmet cuisine as a celebration for the two sisters and their "congregation." As the meal is served, course by course, a miracle of grace slowly unfolds. Gradually the guests begin to settle their differences and forgive one another. While *Babette's Feast* brings many biblical examples and symbols to mind, perhaps its primary lesson is the triumph of grace over religion. It's a story which involves food and fellowship—a physical feast with a spiritual impact.

The Bible is filled with stories and images of festive meals. God ordained a Passover meal for his old covenant people (Exodus 12) as a central part of their memory of salvation from the bondage of Egypt. He provided manna in the wilderness for the nation of Israel (Exodus 16)—a symbol which became reality when Jesus, God in the flesh, pronounced that he was the true bread from heaven (John 6).

The Gospels are filled with examples of banquets and feasts. The first miracle of Jesus was a wedding celebration, when he created wine out of water (John 2). When the prodigal son returned home, his extravagant, loving father who never gave up on him pronounced, *"Bring the fattened calf and kill it. Let's have a feast and celebrate"* (Luke 15:23). At the Last Supper Jesus taught and exemplified what we know now as the Lord's Supper or Communion—a symbol of eating with him and feasting in and of him, now and forever (Matthew 26; Mark 14; Luke 22). The day Jesus was resurrected he walked to Emmaus with two disciples who doubted his resurrection, finally revealing himself to them as they broke bread that evening (Luke 24). In yet another post-resurrection appearance, Jesus made breakfast for his disciples by the Sea of Galilee (John 21).

The king invited everyone to the banquet—no one was excluded. Everyone was welcome!

Two Invitation Lists

The parable we're discussing in this chapter centers around a wedding banquet prepared by a king for his son—and it clearly illustrates the rejection of the son by the king's religious leaders. They rejected the son and his radical new teaching of love, grace and peace. This parable pictures the king sending two invitations to the wedding banquet. The two "invitation lists" effectively included everyone in that culture. The king invited everyone to the banquet—no one was excluded. Everyone was welcome!

Jesus says the first invitation to the wedding banquet (read 'kingdom of heaven') is given to people who refuse the invitation. And they don't just politely refuse—they mistreat and kill the servants who bring the invitation. This first invitation went to "respectable" people—the well-to-do upper class "good" people who seemed, outwardly, to have it all together. People who received the first invitation probably lived in big houses—they were well-educated and well-connected. These people went to established, traditional, affluent, well-endowed churches. But these "respectable" people refused the invitation.

The second invitation was sent out to those who were, as verse nine says, hanging out on the *"street corners."* Let's presume that you are in the middle of planning a wedding for your son or daughter. As you make your invitation list, would you deliberately drive into the wrong/rough side of town, and indiscriminately give invitations to "down on their luck" addicts, drug pushers, criminals and prostitutes to your wedding banquet? No, you wouldn't—and no, I wouldn't. But the king in this parable did.

The people who received this second invitation were not regarded by their society, its culture or its religion, as "respectable." They tended to occupy lower social stations—they tended to be more "working class." The people who received the second invitation included people whose clothing immediately identified them as "second class." The second invitation folks, because of their outward appearance, were not perceived to be as successful or well-connected as the people who received the first invitation.

Grace is always amazing, isn't it? Grace in action always staggers and astounds us. Why invite people to a wedding who are probably going to steal you blind, embarrass you by getting drunk and might even proposition some of your more respectable guests?

It sounds like a crazy thing to do! According to the parable, lots of people who received this second invitation showed up at the wedding banquet. Many of them probably hadn't eaten a good meal in a long time—so they readily accepted the invitation.

The parable of the wedding banquet seems to make two things crystal clear; 1) The king invited everyone to the banquet. No one was excluded. He invited *"the bad as well as the good"* (vs. 10). 2) The big business of religion is center stage in this parable. The first invitation is given to those who had all their doctrinal ducks lined up. The people who received the first invitation felt as if they were doing all the right things. Their spiritual clothing was "in style"—according to the dictates of their religious world. Religious professionals had assured them that their spiritual nakedness was covered by the best spiritual clothing available.

The first invitation crowd knew the fine art of showing up and being seen in the right places at the right time (in church, among other places). The group that received the first invitation spent lots of time going to gatherings, events, ceremonies, celebrations and weddings.

But, in the parable, they refused the invitation, sent by the king, to his son's wedding. They rejected Jesus! Remember, this was no ordinary wedding invitation. This invitation was sent by the king himself! One would have thought this was the event of the year—perhaps of a lifetime for many people.

This parable doesn't mince words as it undeniably illustrates the repudiation and denial of the kingdom of heaven by Christ-less religion and its systems, ceremonies, organizations and institutions. Make no mistake—the kingdom of heaven troubles and threatens the kingdom of religion!

Even though this invitation comes from the king, the religious big-wheel muckedy-mucks turn it down. For that matter, they are so offended and insulted by the king's overture that they mistreat and kill the king's servants who deliver the invitation.

Killing the mailman seems to be a little over the top. Wouldn't it be enough to just call the king's office and tell him you're not coming? Couldn't they have refused to "grace" the banquet with their presence and leave it at that? Some of them did, they *"paid no attention and went off—one to his field, another to his business"*(vs. 5). But *"the rest"* (vs. 6) were so enraged that they killed the messengers.

The king responded by destroying the murderers and burning their city (vs. 7). Does this mean that the king lost his cool and retaliated? No, the parable illustrates the generosity of God. Everyone was invited to the wedding banquet. Everyone. No exceptions. But when those who decided not to attend responded to the king's generosity with hatred and violence, they brought down judgment on their own heads. They had a choice—they chose violence and mayhem over joy and rejoicing.

Ironically (God has a great sense of humor!) the people the religious establishment despised, the people the religious moral guardians wanted no part of, were the very people who were next on the invitation list. Many spend lots of time devising rules designed to keep these "second invitation people" out of their churches. I mean, what's the point of having a religious club if just anyone can be a member?

What kinds of people do religious clubs exclude today? What kinds of people are not welcome in some churches? I'm not going to give you a list—you can come up with your own.

Everyone is Welcome...With One Exception

Once the banquet started, everything seemed to be going well, *"the wedding hall was filled with guests"* (vs. 10), until the king noticed a man who had evidently crashed the party, because he *"was not wearing wedding clothes"* (vs. 11). The king ordered him evicted (vs. 13).

If everyone was welcome at the banquet, why was this poor soul thrown out? If all these low-life people were welcome, why would someone who failed to meet the clothing guidelines get thrown out on his ear? Whoa, looks like everyone is not welcome, after all! Is the king actually enforcing a dress code? Is he insisting that people only wear "approved" spiritual outfits? Does this sound like God's grace?

The point of the parable, in terms of wedding clothing, is that no one who accepted the invitation had the right clothing. Everyone who received the first invitation was informed that they, in spite of how religiously respectable they seemed, could not just show up in their own clothing. Their own spiritual outfits were not good enough. In spite of their presumed ability to buy or rent wedding clothing—they did not have the resources to show up at this wedding in the clothing the king deemed appropriate for this occasion.

The right clothing was clothing that only the king could provide. Everything needed by anyone who was invited would be provided—right down to their clothing. That idea alone must have offended the respected religious leaders. They received the invitation and read the stipulation—"appropriate clothing will be provided" and were scandalized.

"You mean," they sputtered and fumed, "my clothing is not good enough for the king and his son? Well then I'm not going!"

...what's the point of having a religious club if just anyone can be a member?

Their decision to reject Jesus and turn up their righteous noses at the Father's invitation was cemented in their minds when they heard of some of the low class individuals who were invited. That sealed the deal—they didn't want to be seen in the same place or rub elbows with such despicable, unqualified, sordid, pathetic people.

These good "church-going" folks were horrified when they heard about the king inviting both *the bad as well as the good*" (vs. 10). It seemed to them that it didn't matter to the king—he was willing to love and be generous to everyone. And they were right. When God sends out the invitations, they go to everyone. Everyone.

But one of these "first invitation people" did show up, decked out in his own religious outfit. Perhaps the wedding clothing he decided to wear was complete with all kinds of religious medals, merit badges and stripes on the sleeves. It may have looked extremely impressive—something like a five-star religious general might wear. Perhaps the primary reason this man decided to attend the shindig was to show off his spiritual outfit, which he felt was incredibly impressive. Turns out the king wasn't impressed.

The king was absolutely clear—apart from his good graces no one, neither those who received the first invitation nor those who received the second invitation, could purchase or obtain the right clothing. Of course, those who received the second invitation were well aware that they lacked the resources to appear in such an incredibly rich and posh environment that the king would provide for this wedding banquet for his son. The "second invitation people" knew they needed help. They didn't, for a moment, think of showing up in their worn, torn, dirty, moth-eaten, flea-ridden, threadbare spiritual clothing.

We can read more about wedding garments for the wedding of the son—the wedding of Jesus—in the book of Revelation. In Revelation 19:8 we read that the bride of Christ is not expected to go out and buy her own wedding gown—her husband provides it for her. He pays for it with his blood. We also read in Revelation of another imposter who tries to crash the party, wearing clothing she purchases with her own efforts. Revelation 17:4 tells us this imposter is a religious whore—she wears garments she has earned by plying her trade. This passage explains that these garments are considered by God to be *abominable things* and *"the filth of her adulteries."*

And who exactly is this whore who buys her own clothing? Well, Revelation tells us. The whore is a religious imposter who seduces, controls, manipulates and enslaves the world at large.

The lesson of the parable of the wedding banquet is that everyone is welcome. Everyone. There is only one proviso: You don't show up at God's house wearing your own righteousness, or "righteousness" that some religious empire or corporation has given you, in return for your payments, efforts and deeds. You don't show up at the wedding banquet of Jesus wearing what might seem to be a beautiful dress or suit of clothing that you feel you have earned by the sweat of your religious labors. There is no room in the kingdom of heaven for earthly religion, its costumes, habits, outfits and accoutrements.

We either accept the clothing God provides—we either accept his grace—we either accept his Son—we either accept the kingdom of heaven on his terms—or we get thrown out.

We don't pay our own way into the kingdom of heaven. There is no way to honor the Son, no way to accept the invitation, on our terms. There is nothing we can do. We can't buy a ticket—the invitation is free, without charge. We can't get in the back door of the kingdom of heaven as a result of purchasing a pass through a religious power broker.

It doesn't matter how "true" your church is—your church can't give you a pass into the kingdom of heaven. You may belong to one of the many "only true churches" I have run across in my ministry, but that fact means nothing to God. Flashing your membership card from your "only true church" at the door to the wedding banquet will only get you thrown out! Don't try to buy one of those tickets that the ticket scalpers who are standing on the sidewalk just outside the wedding banquet are selling. They're bogus—they're counterfeit—they are absolutely worthless to God. They are nothing but fool's gold.

Many Are Invited—Few Are Chosen

Jesus ends this parable with the saying *"many are invited, but few are chosen"* (vs. 14). Many are invited to follow Jesus, but few are willing to set aside their religious dogmas and traditions. Few are willing to sacrifice their cherished, hallowed, so-called "holy" ceremonies and rituals to follow Jesus. Few are willing to wear the spiritual clothing he alone can provide. Many reject the Son because few are willing to lose their religious heritage, legacy and tradition in order to follow him.

There is only one way into the kingdom of heaven. There is only one door. His name is Jesus. There's only one way to have Jesus. We must accept him on his terms, and the terms are called "God's grace." God's grace or nothing. God's grace or the highway.

We do not deserve Jesus because of our church membership. We do not deserve Jesus because we believe in and regularly recite the right creeds. We do not deserve Jesus because God is obligated to reward us for our dutiful and careful obedience. That is the big lie of organized religion. Our obedience cannot purchase the required wedding clothing. God already has all of the obedience he needs—it was given on the cross of Christ. Our wedding clothing has been purchased by the blood of Christ.

When Jesus says *"many"* are invited, but few are chosen, the Greek for *"many"* is inclusive. It means "virtually everyone"—this *"many"* is not restrictive. Everyone is welcome.

God is not a respecter of persons. The invitation to his banquet in the kingdom of heaven is not just to the powerful, well-connected, famous, righteous or courageous. The invitation is given to the least, the lost and the last. God invites losers!

When Jesus says *"few are chosen"* he means few choose to respond to the invitation and thus many are not chosen. After all, everyone is invited. Like most invitations, this wedding invitation has an R.S.V.P. The king's invitation is an open invitation, with the proviso that acceptance means that we accept on his terms. To R.S.V.P. means, among other things, that we surrender

> ...your church can't give you a pass into the kingdom of heaven.

our spiritual pride and allow God to do for us what we cannot do for ourselves. It means accepting the reality that we are unable to pay our own way, spiritually. It means that we are not free to accept the king's invitation and then attend the wedding on our terms.

The king doesn't offer the option of wearing the shoes he provides, while offering guests the option to choose their own shirt and tie—or dress or undergarments. It's God's way or no way. It's *faith alone, grace alone and Christ alone*—religion is not an option. Of course the very idea that we are absolutely buck naked, spiritually speaking, and unable to clothe ourselves with our good deeds is humiliating. But humility is one of the central planks of the kingdom of heaven.

We are not free to accept his invitation and then add a list of religious innovations, regulations, restrictions, duties and deeds. He wants us to come to the wedding banquet of his Son, but we must come only on his terms—only by and through his grace.

One Christian ministry (highly respected in North America) once said "Whether or not we reach heaven depends totally on our obedience."

When it comes to qualifying for his kingdom of heaven—when it comes to earning a ticket into the heavenly wedding banquet of his Son—according to the book of Revelation, God sees the harvest of religion as *"abominable things"* (Revelation 17:4). Our efforts to spiritually clothe and adorn ourselves are but filthy rags in comparison to the one and only way we may receive his kingdom—the riches of his grace.

> **WE ARE ALL INVITED TO THE HEAD TABLE. THERE ARE NO OTHER TABLES—JUST THE MAIN TABLE. ALL SEATS AT THE KING'S BANQUET ARE EQUAL.**

The idea that reaching heaven depends totally on our obedience is absolute *de facto* evidence that performance-based legalism runs roughshod in Christendom, seducing and deceiving many into thinking that they can earn their way into the kingdom of heaven. Think about that statement again— "Whether or not we reach heaven depends totally on our obedience." According to the parable of the wedding banquet, those who arrive at the wedding of the son wearing their own obedience are kicked to the heavenly curb—thrown out on their ear.

There is something else about this parable we need to note. This parable is but one of many references in the New Testament that characterizes God's kingdom of heaven as unmitigated joy—a banquet, a celebration, a party.

The kingdom of heaven involves feasting and dancing and laughter. God—God the Father, God the Son, and God the Holy Spirit—does not absent himself from such merrymaking. God is involved in the wining and the dining—he is the very center of the joke telling, the good natured jesting, the singing and the offering of toasts. This is his banquet—he plans it, caters it and hosts it. God doesn't absent himself from the party and sneak off to the library, reading the Bible in the original Greek or Hebrew. God is right there in the middle of all the festivities.

The heavenly wedding banquet is a love feast where everyone is welcome. There are no strangers in the kingdom of heaven. There are no second class citizens. There is no backroom where the likes of you and I will be shown a dingy table, right next to the noise of the kitchen, where we will be served scraps and leftovers. We are all invited to the head table. There are no other tables—just the main table. All the seats at the king's banquet are equal. Everyone receives the same rich fare, the riches of God's grace, the new wine of the new covenant, the Bread of Life—the very life of our Lord and Savior.

The wedding banquet of the Son is a time of delight and joy—as long as we accept the Father's invitation, and receive the Son, on God's terms, by his grace.

CHAPTER 2

The Great Reversal

"For the kingdom of heaven is like a landowner who went out early in the morning to hire workers for his vineyard. He agreed to pay them a denarius for the day and sent them into his vineyard.

About nine in the morning he went out and saw others standing in the marketplace doing nothing. He told them, 'You also go and work in my vineyard, and I will pay you whatever is right.' So they went.

He went out again about noon and about three in the afternoon and did the same thing. About five in the afternoon he went out and found still others standing around. He asked them, 'Why have you been standing here all day long doing nothing?'

'Because no one has hired us,' they answered.

He said to them, 'You also go and work in my vineyard.'

When evening came, the owner of the vineyard said to his foreman, 'Call the workers and pay them *their wages, beginning with the last ones hired and going on to the first.'*

The workers who were hired about five in the afternoon came and each received a denarius. So when those came who were hired first, they expected to receive more. But each one of them also received a denarius. When they received it, they began to grumble against the landowner. 'These who were hired last worked only one hour,' they said, 'and you have made them equal to us who have borne the burden of the work and the heat of the day.'

But he answered one of them, 'I am not being unfair to you, friend. Didn't you agree to work for a denarius? Take your pay and go. I want to give the one who was hired last the same as I gave you. Don't I have the right to do what I want with my own money? Or are you envious because I am generous?'

So the last will be first, and the first will be last."
—Matthew 20:1-16

According to a paper presented at the annual convention of the American Psychological Association in 2000, "Show me the money!" (from the movie *Jerry Maguire*) is one of the most popular movie quotations of all time. "Show me the money" is not only similar to the physical demands of many churches, it's also the spiritual motto of the kingdom of religion. All who are incarcerated in the kingdom of religion are encouraged to regularly check their spiritual ledgers and statements which record their good behaviors, rituals performed, prayers said, creeds memorized, Scriptures read, ceremonies fulfilled, good deeds done and church services attended (where there are, of course, guilt-ridden and shame-based exhortations to write checks from physical bank accounts payable to the church!).

Prison guards in the kingdom of religion function as spiritual bookkeepers. Spiritual prisoners exist in a perpetual state of bankruptcy. Inmates in the kingdom of religion never have enough good deeds deposited in their bank account. No matter how hard they work—no matter how much overtime they put in—it's never enough.

By contrast, God's grace is the currency, the spiritual economy, of the kingdom of heaven. Deposits in the bank of heaven are unlimited. There is no end to the riches of the kingdom of heaven. One of the many differences between the kingdom of religion and the kingdom of heaven is that those who are free in Christ don't receive regular statements of their bank balances. In the kingdom of heaven, there is never any need to balance the assets of your good deeds against the liabilities of your bad behaviors in a monthly bank statement, because in the kingdom of heaven we live by faith, not by sight (2 Corinthians 5:7).

The fear of the unknown is but one of the many objections humans have to God's grace. Living by faith is a frightening proposition, because grace causes the mirage of spiritual security offered by the kingdoms of religion to disappear. The spiritual economy of the kingdom of heaven frightens us, because we can't control it.

God's grace is not traded on religious currency exchanges. God's grace can't be counted or quantified. Whereas the kingdom of religion insists on forever reminding us that we are spiritually bankrupt, and offering us regular proof of our inadequacy, God's grace defies religious bean counters. God's grace cannot be calculated, computed or comprehended by Christ-less religion.

God's grace is beyond human control. We can't organize it, we can't put in the barn and we can't build a fence around it—it's free.

"It is for freedom that Christ has set us free. Stand firm, then, and do not let yourselves be burdened again with a yoke of slavery" (Galatians 5:1).

Grace is freedom in Christ. It's *God's favor, given freely* to those who give up their religious counterfeit currency, surrender to him, and live, in faith.

A little over a year ago, as a result of some unexpected expenses, I drove to a bank a mile or so from our home. This bank was the place where my wife and I kept an interest-bearing "emergency fund" and it was time to withdraw some funds. As I was making the withdrawal a bank employee asked if we could sit down and talk. She explained that if I withdrew that amount my account would fall below a minimal level, and that I would incur "service charges." I asked the specific amount of the "service charges" and when she divulged them I quickly "did the numbers." I concluded that if I left the remaining money in this bank, then the insignificant interest they would pay me would not keep pace with the "service charges." I would be paying them to keep my money!

I calmly, but firmly, informed the bank employee that if they insisted on inflicting those "service charges" I would then close my account, and if necessary, in this era of virtually no interest, hide the money under my mattress! She didn't get my humor (not everyone does!). She seemed to take my tongue-in-cheek threat to hide the money under my mattress literally. She took a long look at me, as if I were like Gulliver, just waking up from a long sleep and arriving in the 21st-century. Then, seeing she simply had a feisty old coot on her hands, after a brief discussion, she came up with a way that I would not have to pay the service charges. As I suspected, when push came to shove, though our emergency savings account is small, the bank didn't want to lose our money.

As I drove home I reflected on the spiritual significance of this encounter. In our world, whether it's the workplace or the church, the relationship others are willing to have with you is normally based on a bottom line. The relationship you have with a bank is based on the money you have on deposit. If your checkbook doesn't balance, you are an undesirable. You must maintain a minimum balance. In the spiritual realm, many are led to believe that if they don't show up at church often enough the religious bankers will start adding service charges to their account—or just show them the door that supposedly leads directly to eternal torture in hell. The kingdom of religion is a world of un-grace.

But God's grace storms into the world of Christless religion and defies the religious bankers. God's grace turns the world of spiritual bookkeeping upside down. God's grace is truly good news because it declares that our relationship with God is not about our ongoing efforts to maintain a minimal balance!

Those of us who live by God's grace believe it is sufficient to meet our needs. Those of us who live in God's grace don't receive actual kingdom of heaven banknotes we can see and touch and feel and carry in our purses and wallets—and for that reason the kingdom of heaven scares people. Some even believe that the currency of grace in the kingdom of heaven is "funny money"—they seem to regard grace as almost fictitious, on the basis that it cannot be scientifically measured, weighed and tested. They are troubled because the kingdom of heaven doesn't send monthly statements to let them know "how they're doing."

Because they feel more comfortable with religious progress reports many feel threatened by God's grace and prefer conducting their spiritual business in the kingdom of religion. After all, the kingdom of religion has a currency which can be touched, seen, felt, measured, counted and proven—by human instruments and methods.

A Parable About Workers?

Many translations of the Bible present Matthew 20:1-16 as a parable about workers. But it would be more accurate to say that this parable is about God and how he relates to workers. That the parable is about God, not us, should be obvious from the first words—*"For the kingdom of heaven is like a landowner..."* (vs. 1).

We can all relate to stories about workers, can't we? After all, the vast majority of us are still workers in our daily lives, to one degree or another. You might be retired or semi-retired, but you still relate to the world of work. We all have our stories about the workplace, and Jesus offers us this classic. It is one of my favorites among all his parables.

The landowner has a job that needs to be done, so he continues to hire workers until he is satisfied that the work will get done. From a worker's perspective, one of the most, if not the most, important of all facets of the workplace is the wage. What do I get for my efforts? So it is that the lesson of this parable hinges around payday.

The reason God's grace is so offensive to the religious mindset is that it does not compute. *Grace doesn't make sense!* It doesn't add up. We, after all, can count. We know how long we have worked, and we also know how long and hard others have worked. All we want is for our employer to be fair. This parable is offensive because it doesn't line up with our sense of fair play. How in the world can the role assigned to the landowner of this parable be played by God?

JESUS, THE KING OF THE KINGDOM OF HEAVEN, IS THE KING WHO TRIUMPHS by LOSING, WHO IS VICTORIOUS THROUGH THE HUMILIATION OF THE CROSS AND WHO SERVES by dying.

Again—this parable is not about the workers. It is about God and his kingdom. It's a parable about God, and how he "works," and it's a parable about how his kingdom "works." The first words of this parable tell us that this parable is about the kingdom of heaven, not about any kingdoms of our world, religious or secular. This parable describes the fundamental nature of God's kingdom—and it does so by turning the tables, by turning expectations and values upside down. This parable is a great reversal.

To use a baseball metaphor, the teachings of Jesus were somewhat like Jesus being on the mound, pitching parables to the religious world of his day. In baseball parlance, Jesus' parables are "junk" pitches that keep the religious opposition off balance. Time and again Jesus throws curve balls, knuckle balls, sliders and change-ups. He confounds religious expectations. That's one of the reasons that religion then, and now, is not all that fond of Jesus. Religion can't "hit" Jesus.

William Temple, who was the physical leader of the Church of England before his death in World War 2, once gave an illustration of how God's kingdom turns the kingdoms of this world, and their values and their expectations, upside down. He used the illustration of a small English shop or store with room for only one big display window. The shop displays its goods in the window so that window shoppers can examine the items for sale and their asking price.

Using the illustration of a shop window, William Temple said something like this (forgive my paraphrase): "Apart from God, the world as we know it is like a shop. A mischievous person has broken into the shop overnight—and rearranged the items in the shop window, shifting all the high price labels so that the cheap things now have high prices, and the really precious things have price labels that define them as inexpensive, inferior and even worthless."

In Luke 16:15 Jesus, speaking to the religious leaders of his day, told them that they had effectively changed all the price tags in God's kingdom: *"What people highly value is detestable in God's sight."*

It's relatively easy to think of our world at large and see its physical values as topsy-turvy—upside down from God's values. But in the parable of the workers Jesus was not primarily addressing the secular values of materialism and money—he was addressing religious ideas about the kingdom of heaven. He was talking about religious practices within what we today know as Christendom as being out of step with God's values. Luke says the values of the kingdom of religion are "...*detestable in God's sight.*"

Jesus introduces this parable, as he does many others, with the familiar words *"the kingdom of heaven is like..."* (Matthew 20:1). It's a parable of a great reversal—about how the kingdom of God turns the values of the kingdoms of this world upside down.

The Upside Down Kingdom

The phrase "upside down kingdom" was popularized by Donald Kraybill in his 1978 book, *The Upside Down Kingdom*. Kraybill pointed out that Jesus, the king of the kingdom of heaven, is the king who triumphs by losing, who is victorious through the humiliation of the cross and who serves by dying. The kingdom of heaven 1) seeks out, serves and gives grace to the lost, the least and the last, 2) opposes religious scorekeepers who meticulously record both good and bad behavior, and 3) turns the kingdoms of religion upside down and every which way but loose. In Matthew chapter 20 we read that:

• Jesus taught how the first in earthly kingdoms are last in his kingdom, and the last according to score-keeping religious dogmas and doctrines are first in the kingdom of heaven (Matthew 20:16).

• Jesus came to serve, rather than to be served (Matthew 20:28), explaining that those who are truly great in the kingdom of heaven are those who become, by God's gracious transformation, servants as he was and is.

The life and teachings of Jesus are a great reversal—a truly upside down kingdom! Though Jesus was God in the flesh, his earthly life was one of humility and sacrifice. He was born into a blue-collar, working class family, and was specifically born in a barnyard, surrounded by animals. Shepherds, whose profession was regarded by that culture as among the lowest of the low, were the first to be invited to visit the newborn Jesus—and they accepted the invitation! Mary was an unmarried teenager when the Holy Spirit overshadowed her (Luke 1:35), impregnating her with Immanuel—God with us (Matthew 1:23).

Jesus *"...made himself nothing by taking the very nature of a servant..."* (Philippians 2:7) so that he might become one of us. Paul tells us:

"For you know the grace of our Lord Jesus Christ, that though he was rich, yet for your sake he became poor, so that you through his poverty might become rich" (2 Corinthians 8:9).

In his teachings and parables Jesus chose despised Samaritans, money-grubbing tax collectors and untrustworthy shepherds as heroes, rather than highly esteemed, church-going rules-keeping religious types. Jesus' attention was focused on lepers and prostitutes more than the worldly wisdom of respected priests and teachers of the law. He reached out to children and women—he touched the "unclean."

Christ-less religion values church-ianity without Christ. It values religious rituals and regulations without grace. It has swapped the price tags. Legalism is highly valued, and God's grace is seen as anemic and feeble. Many infected with the virus of legalism believe if grace and love are the final words then the gospel is spineless sentimentalism.

Christ-less religion values those who earn their own way, who work hard—those who build impressive buildings and call those buildings a church or cathedral dedicated to God.

But God says, in Isaiah 66:1, *"Heaven is my throne, and the earth is my footstool. Where is the house you will build for me?"*

Religious institutions are often looking, like the U.S. Army, for a few good, strong men. Churches often view people in need as a drag on their resources, whereas the young, strong and financially secure are highly coveted. But Jesus is looking for the person who has either been physically or spiritually beaten and left for dead, ignored by religious leaders—to whom he, the despised Good Samaritan, can minister.

Jesus is looking for lepers to cleanse, prostitutes and addicts of all kinds to lift out of their lives of bondage, and for those who are afflicted with all kinds of diseases—both physical and especially spiritual—so that he may heal them. This is the very ministry of Jesus, for he himself is described by the prophet Isaiah, in 53:3, as being *"despised and rejected by mankind."*

Paul tells us in 2 Corinthians 12:10:

"That is why, for Christ's sake, I delight in weaknesses, in insults, in hardships, in persecutions, in difficulties. For when I am weak, then I am strong."

Religious institutions delight in huge church buildings, with expensive stained glass installations, with highly involved rituals and ceremonies and ornate traditions and clothing for religious leaders. Established religious institutions often despise those who do not frequent their church buildings, who do not perform their religious ceremonies or honor their religious traditions.

Big business religion reviles those who do not march to a religious drum beat, who do not recite denominational creeds and who do not line up their theological, doctrinal ducks in the order that the religious establishment says they must.

Christians, who are the church, by virtue of the life Christ lives in them, but determine not to attend a brick and mortar church, and who do not pray memorized prayers or sing accepted songs out of a religiously ordained hymnal, are often disregarded or judged to be "unsaved" or "unbelievers"— or, at best, "lazy slackers. "

God is so good that he pours out his love on us, not because we merit or deserve it, but because he loves to love us.

In our parable, Jesus tells us that what God does with his grace is none of our business. Who exactly the landowner chooses, precisely who is invited into his vineyard, and when, and under what terms is his business, not ours! In the great reversal, Jesus uses money as a picture of God's grace—the way in which he invites people into his kingdom.

Jesus concludes this parable by saying, *"Can't I do what I want with my own money? Are you going to get stingy because I am generous?"* (Matthew 20:15, *The Message,* by Eugene Peterson).

God's kingdom is a great reversal of the kingdoms of our world and its kingdoms of religion. Our world and its religion works on the principle that if you do something for God (or rather, religion), then God will respond and do something for you.

Christ-less religion persuades its followers that if they please God he will reward them. Churchianity presents and explains God, the landowner, as a divine potentate who pays us for services we render to him, rewarding us with blessings in return for good, hard, dedicated work and cursing us for lazy, sinful behavior.

The theme of the great reversal is foundational to the gospel of the kingdom:

"For the wages of sin is death, but the gift of God is eternal life in Christ Jesus our Lord" (Romans 6:23).

The only thing we are capable of earning is death. Note that Romans 6:23 does not say "the punishment of God when you sin is death." The good news is that the gift of God is eternal life through Jesus Christ our Lord.

A gift is not something we earn—otherwise it is not a gift, but a purchase. The point of the parable of the great reversal is simply this: God is so good that he pours out his love on us, not because we merit or deserve it, but because *he loves to love us*. He invites us into his vineyard, not because he needs us to do what he is otherwise powerless to do, but because he invites us to participate in his kingdom. The great reversal is all about the extravagant goodness of God.

"All Is Forgiven—Love, Papa"

Then Peter came to Jesus and asked, "Lord, how many times shall I forgive my brother or sister who sins against me? Up to seven times?"

Jesus answered, "I tell you, not seven times, but seventy-seven times.

Therefore, the kingdom of heaven is like a king who wanted to settle accounts with his servants. As he began the settlement, a man who owed him ten thousand bags of gold was brought to him. Since he was not able to pay, the master ordered that he and his wife and his children and all that he had be sold to repay the debt.

At this the servant fell on his knees before him. 'Be patient with me,' he begged, 'and I will pay back everything.' The servant's master took pity on him, canceled the debt and let him go.

But when that servant went out, he found one of his fellow servants who owed him a hundred silver coins. He grabbed him and began to choke him. 'Pay back what you owe me!' he demanded.

His fellow servant fell to his knees and begged him, 'Be patient with me, and I will pay it back.'

But he refused. Instead, he went off and had the man thrown into prison until he could pay the debt. When the other servants saw what had happened, they were outraged and went and told their master everything that had happened.

Then the master called the servant in. 'You wicked servant,' he said, 'I canceled all that debt of yours because you begged me to. Shouldn't you have had mercy on your fellow servant just as I had on you?' In anger his master handed him over to the jailers to be tortured, until he should pay back all he owed.

This is how my heavenly Father will treat each of you unless you forgive your brother or sister from your heart."—Matthew 18:21-35

In his story, "The Capital of the World," Ernest Hemingway wrote about a Spanish father who wanted to be reconciled with his son. His son had run away to the lights and attractions of the big city of Madrid. The father put an advertisement in the newspaper: "Paco, meet me at the Hotel Montana at noon on Tuesday. All is forgiven! Love, Papa."

Paco is a common name in Spain—so much so that when the father went to the Hotel Montana on Tuesday at noon, there were 800 young men named Paco waiting for their fathers!

We all desperately crave forgiveness! Our hunger for forgiveness and reconciliation is one of the most basic of all human desires and yearnings. But while we desperately seek forgiveness for ourselves, we often seem reluctant to see others receive it. While we long to be forgiven, we find forgiving those who, as so many country-and-western or blues songs express, "done us wrong," to be extremely difficult. There are so many songs about people doing each other wrong that some years ago one popular song was called "Another Somebody Done Somebody Wrong Song."

The fact that we all crave forgiveness is one of the reasons why the gospel is such incredibly good news! Can you imagine the gospel of Jesus Christ without forgiveness? Can you imagine experiencing God's grace without being forgiven? Forgiveness lies at the heart of our relationship with God. There is no reconciliation without forgiveness.

This parable of Jesus is often referred to as the parable of the unforgiving servant. It's a parable about someone who had been forgiven much yet ironically finds himself unwilling to forgive someone who owes him a comparatively small sum. This is a parable of unimaginable forgiveness—forgiveness that defies human logic—forgiveness that seems, to the human mind, apart from God's grace, like a fairy tale.

The parable of the unforgiving servant follows a conversation between Peter and Jesus and the answer Jesus gives to Peter's question. Peter wants to know how many times he is required to forgive—is there a limit when he can stop forgiving? Peter suggests seven would be a good number to use as a limitation on forgiveness. After all, what if someone takes advantage of the opportunity to be forgiven—and keeps misbehaving, continually requesting forgiveness? Surely Jesus isn't saying that we should just keep on forgiving, no matter what?

Jesus responds with a deliberate hyperbolic exaggeration. He tells Peter that he should forgive seventy times seven times. Jesus is saying, of course, that there is no end to forgiveness. The forgiveness God gives has no boundaries. Jesus is saying that divine forgiveness is not an exercise in bookkeeping. The forgiveness that comes from God does not depend on accurate record keeping. Paul says a similar thing when he writes about the love of God, in 1 Corinthians 13:5:

"It does not dishonor others, it is not self-seeking, it is not easily angered, it keeps no record of wrongs."

Forgiveness Without Limits

After Jesus says God's forgiveness has no limits, then he begins the parable of the unforgiving servant. Jesus begins this parable with the same introduction he uses for a number of other parables, by saying: *"the kingdom of heaven is like…"* The kingdom of heaven is like this story—the kingdom of heaven is filled with forgiveness, it is a kingdom of mercy and grace.

Jesus begins the parable with law. In what is perhaps his most detailed parable about forgiveness, Jesus describes a debtor who owes ten thousand bags of gold being brought to his king. The king is a spiritual accountant—a spiritual bean counter. For that reason alone, regardless of the mercy this king later gives, we should hesitate before deciding that Jesus is casting God the Father in the role of this king. While we might understand some of the actions of the king of this parable as God-like, this character is not a perfect reflection of our heavenly Father. Our loving heavenly Father does not keep a record of our debts. The love of God *"…keeps no record of wrongs"* (1 Corinthians 13:5).

As the story begins, the debtor, who owes ten thousand bags of gold (earlier translations defined the debt as being ten thousand talents), is brought before the king, who wants to settle accounts. It's difficult to translate a generic reference to 10,000 bags of gold or talents into today's currency. Interpretations differ about how much this amount actually is.

One writer suggested that the average working man in the first-century would have needed to work for twenty years to earn one talent. If that estimate is accurate, we're talking about this man's debt being roughly equivalent to 200,000 years of work. Considering that most people are able to work about 40 years in their lifetime today, the debt owed by the debtor was equal to the total earnings of 5,000 lifetimes!

The point of the parable, of course, is not the exact amount that he owed. The most recent, 2011 revision of the New International Version recognizes this issue, and uses the far less precise "bags of gold" rather than talents (for more about bags of gold versus talents please see Chapter Six). By a hyperbolic exaggeration Jesus has already stipulated that a precise number of times we must forgive someone is not the issue. By the same token, Jesus is not giving us the exact amount this debtor owed. He is instead illustrating the stupendous debt of spiritual bankruptcy that this man (and any human for that matter) owes. No one could ever, in 5,000 lifetimes, repay this debt!

By the way, this debtor is someone who had been given some degree of responsibility. After all, not everyone would have the capabilities necessary to run up this kind of incredible debt! When the debtor is faced with the staggering consequences of his debt—he cannot repay his debt and he and his wife and his family will all become slaves to help pay off that debt—he throws himself on the mercy of the king.

But a truly amazing thing happens! The king forgives the debt! All the debtor has to do to receive grace is to recognize his inability to repay his debt and request forgiveness from the king!

This unforgiving forgiven debtor is you and me—and all humanity! We are programmed to default to living by law—by records—by counting the sins and grievances of everyone who owes us.

Even more amazing, even though the debtor doesn't seem to realize it, is that full and complete forgiveness is given without any strings attached. There are no preconditions. There is no contract to sign. There is no collateral the debtor must provide, nor any down payment (earnest money) he must pay up front as an evidence of his intent. There is no schedule of repayments—no obligation to repay a certain number of talents each month.

The king cancels the debt for no obvious reason. The king cancels the debt because he can, and of course in this regard we might say that he is like our loving God who unconditionally forgives us. God forgives for no humanly perceived apparent reason! God's forgiveness is given to those who have proven themselves virtually useless—completely unable to keep their own spiritual houses in order!

50

But the debtor who had failed so miserably (like all human beings) just can't believe the king's unconditional grace (failure to believe the riches of God's grace is another all-too-human trait!). The king doesn't stipulate repayment, but the debtor decides he needs to salvage some self-respect and attempt some token repayment. Driven by the desire to save face, the debtor certainly can't see any direct correlation to the lavish, unheard of forgiveness he has just received to the forgiveness he can, in turn, pass on to others. In order to repay the king, the recently forgiven servant, having been forgiven a debt that it would take him 5,000 lifetimes to repay, turns around and refuses to forgive someone who owed him the equivalent of $50.

The forgiven debtor is still operating out of his old religious paradigm. In spite of the grace lavished on him, he is still working on the basis of his own self-salvation program. He is like the prodigal son who planned to be a slave for his father so that he could recoup the inheritance he squandered. Grace was too absurd to consider.

The forgiven debtor failed to respond to someone who begged him to forgive them, someone who used *the exact same words* he himself used when he begged the king for his own forgiveness. He failed to feel pity because he was so absorbed in trying to find a way to repay his own debt! Jesus sets up this scene so that we, his listeners and readers, would naturally be appalled and wonder why the callous, insensitive much-forgiven man would not forgive someone who owed him a comparatively insignificant amount.

This unforgiving forgiven debtor is you and me —and all humanity! We are programmed to default to living by law—by numbers, calculations and amounts—by counting the sins of everyone who owes us. Unless we unreservedly embrace the grace which God gives us, we are incapable of passing it on to others. Unless we fully embrace the grace of God, we wind up biting the hand of the One who spiritually feeds us! Until we fully embrace God's grace, we will never fully realize the extravagant, unheard of, beyond belief grace we have been given.

Forgiven Yet Unforgiving!

The forgiven servant who was himself unforgiving is every man and every woman—in the sense that 1) we love to experience grace ourselves, but we are loathe to pass it on to others—in fact we often begrudge grace when others receive it, and 2) God's grace just seems to be too good to be true—so much so that even when he lavishes his grace on us our attention and focus almost always reverts back to legalistic record keeping.

Similar scenes happen all the time when God's amazing, staggering, radical grace is preached. Even though God's grace is the very heart and core of the gospel of Jesus Christ, when the real implications of God's grace are explained, objections resound throughout the world of Christendom.

When a pastor preaches about grace, many in the congregation, especially the board of deacons and others in positions of authority, insist on a series of sermons the next few weeks to "balance out" the sermon about grace. "After all," so goes the thinking, "if we just preach grace and leave it at that, people might get the wrong idea. If we just leave them with this 'grace thing' how in the world can we control them?"

So after a grace sermon or two is given the call goes out for sermons about laws, obedience, accountability, standards, requirements of church membership, about the obligation to attend church every Sunday and of course about the necessity to pay a ten-percent tithe, no matter what. Immediately following any discussion of grace many people demand sermons about judgment and eternal torture in hell—these sermons, it would seem, are directed toward those who might be tempted to go overboard and take God's love, grace and forgiveness far more seriously than they "should."

Here are some actual statements made in sermons or in written form by those who claim their teaching is based on the teachings of Jesus Christ:

- Your forgiveness is guaranteed *as long as* you forgive others.
- You must forgive *if* you expect to be forgiven.
- God will not forgive you *unless and until* you forgive others.

God's limitless, unconditional forgiveness, given by his grace, based on his love, scares people. God's amazing forgiveness rocks religious boats—it disturbs the religious status quo—it upsets religious apple carts—it turns the values of Christ-less religion upside down. Christ-less religion is deathly afraid of losing control, and so are we, for that matter. If we accept God's grace, then we know that we are in his good graces. But wait!

While we like the idea of being in God's good graces, we don't like the process of getting there—for God insists that we can only arrive in his good graces as a consequence of his free gift.

There's the rub! We humans do not like the humility involved in accepting handouts.

When God offers us his grace, without cost and without strings, it frightens us. We don't want to accept his free handouts—so we, like the servant who owed 5,000 lifetimes of work, often prefer to revert to religious record keeping. We reject grace because we actually prefer to count our own sins and the sins of others, even though God refuses to do so. This is the judgment that Jesus says we bring on ourselves.

The parable concludes with the master (the king) handing over the man who had been forgiven much, yet who refused to forgive a small amount, to jailors who would torture him.

Upon reading this last part of the parable many who are themselves confused (like the unforgiving servant was) by God's lavish grace, say, "You see what happens? God will send us to hell if we don't do all the right things—don't give me this grace stuff!"

This same chapter of Matthew 18 records the parable of the lost sheep. This parable concludes: *"In the same way your Father in heaven is not willing that any of these little ones should perish"* (Matthew 18:14).

Are we to assume that Jesus, who is *"...the same yesterday, today and forever"* (Hebrews 13:8) is telling us that the Father who, in Matthew 18:14, was not willing that any should perish, is depicted, 18 verses later (vs. 32) as torturing the hell out of those who are unmerciful? Is God threatening to torture us unless we are merciful?

God is not willing that anyone should perish. God is not willing that anyone be lost in hopeless debt that he can never repay. God is not willing to leave anyone in the horrible delusion that he can bail himself out of a bottomless pit. God is not willing to lose anyone, even those who are so enslaved by performance-based religion that they cannot recognize the pleas for mercy they hear from others as being the exact same pleas they themselves utter before the King.

Is God planning to torture us for being unmerciful? No, the parable simply says that the master (whether or not Jesus is casting God the Father in this role is not absolutely clear) allows us to choose our own destiny. In this parable, the master doesn't send anyone to hell. Neither does God.

Jesus ends this parable by saying there are those who refuse to accept grace and forgiveness—and by doing so, they insist on living in a dog-eat-dog religious world where each and every sin must be paid for. Those who resist divine forgiveness will insist on Christ-less religion, living their lives enslaved by spiritual accountants and bean-counters. They have a choice.

The master in the parable reluctantly accepts the decision of those who insist on remaining lost in a graceless world. He simply states the obvious—those who cut themselves off from the grace that is offered to them will live with the religious nightmare they choose, the spiritual torture they will endure in a graceless world. Living in a state of unforgiveness is torture. If we choose to live in religious bondage, we choose the consequences of seemingly endless, unforgiving shame and guilt. God doesn't impose this state—we choose it!

Jesus ends this parable by saying if we live by the sword of legalism, if we refuse to experience the rest and peace that God offers, then we choose to die by the sword of legalism. God does not actively mete out punishment, he does not fuel the cycle of legalism, but he does not stand in the way of those who insist on remaining within the prison cells of Christ-less religion.

The king in this story, who is not one and the same as our loving heavenly Father in every way (as I mentioned earlier), simply allows the servant who was forgiven an incredible debt, and in turn refused to forgive a debt of $50, to live in bondage to Christ-less religion. You may have heard the maxim or proverb: "I do not have the right to deny you the consequences of your actions."

Parents learn this lesson as their children mature and grow. Regardless of what we as parents do or do not do, children will eventually make their own choices. There are times when we as parents are delighted with our mature children's choices, and there are times when we are bewildered and even appalled. But as our children grow and mature and assume their place in society, we come to realize that we cannot deny them the consequences of their choices.

In some respects, while the king in this story is not identical to God, and while earthly parents are not identical with our heavenly Father, our Father God takes a similar perspective regarding our choices. God does not force his grace and forgiveness on anyone. Divine forgiveness is available to all, without cost—but we are not compelled to receive it. The decision about accepting his forgiveness is ours.

If we accept his forgiveness we will, by definition, pass that forgiveness on to others. We will pass it on to others because the act of accepting his forgiveness means accepting the risen life of Jesus, so that *"I no longer live, but Christ lives in me"* (Galatians 2:20). When Jesus lives within us, he will, sooner or later, in his time and his way, produce an attitude of forgiveness for others.

Those who fail to forgive themselves or others are actually saying that their standard of forgiveness is higher than that of God's, for they fail to realize or accept that God has already forgiven their own sins and those who have sinned against them.

God does not actively mete out punishment, he does not fuel the cycle of legalism, but he does not stand in the way of those who insist on remaining within the prison cells of Christ-less religion.

Really letting go of what we believe we deserve and what we believe others owe us is hard to do. In fact, it's impossible apart from God's grace. We cannot fully receive God's grace unless and until we reject self-salvation schemes, religious self-justification programs and merciless spiritual scorekeeping (of our performance as well as that of others). His forgiveness creates forgiveness in us. The message of the gospel is truly amazing. It's summed up in a message to you and me from our heavenly Father: "All is forgiven—Love, Papa."

CHAPTER 4

A Tale of Two Nobodies

On one occasion an expert in the law stood up to test Jesus. "Teacher," he asked, "what must I do to inherit eternal life?"

"What is written in the Law?" he replied. "How do you read it?"

He answered, "'Love the Lord your God with all your heart and with all your soul and with all your strength and with all your mind'; and, 'Love your neighbor as yourself.'"

"You have answered correctly," Jesus replied. "Do this and you will live."

But he wanted to justify himself, so he asked Jesus, "And who is my neighbor?"

In reply Jesus said: "A man was going down from Jerusalem to Jericho, when he was attacked by robbers. They stripped him of his clothes, beat him and went away, leaving him half dead. A priest happened to be going down the same road, and when he saw the man, *he passed by on the other side. So too, a Levite, when he came to the place and saw him, passed by on the other side. But a Samaritan, as he traveled, came where the man was; and when he saw him, he took pity on him. He went to him and bandaged his wounds, pouring on oil and wine. Then he put the man on his own donkey, brought him to an inn and took care of him. The next day he took out two denarii and gave them to the innkeeper. 'Look after him,' he said, 'and when I return, I will reimburse you for any extra expense you may have.'*

"Which of these three do you think was a neighbor to the man who fell into the hands of robbers?" The expert in the law replied, "The one who had mercy on him." Jesus told him, "Go and do likewise."—Luke 10:25-37

Reading Jesus' parables often reminds me of the words Forrest Gump credited to his mother: "Life is like a box of chocolates. You never know what you're gonna get." Many sermons about the parable of the Good Samaritan interpret this story as a morality tale, based on the last verse *"Go and do likewise."* But such interpretations ignore the other chocolates in the box, and leave the rich delights of unexpected grace untasted.

Several decades ago a professor in a seminary assigned a sermon based on the Good Samaritan to his preachers-in-training. As a part of their final exam, each student was given the task of preparing a sermon and then delivering it in front of the professor and a videotape operator. After the sermon was delivered, the professor could replay portions of the sermon and thereby help the student improve.

But this was not the only videotaping the homiletics professor had in mind.

Without telling his students, the professor arranged for an actor to play the part of the brutalized, half-dead man who was left by the side of the road in Jesus' parable. Each student was assigned a specific time during the day when their sermon would be taped. The professor arranged for the actor to be lying on the sidewalk only a few feet outside the classroom, ensuring that each preacher-in-training, en route to deliver a sermon about the Good Samaritan, would encounter a bloodied, beaten and mugged person. The professor also arranged for a hidden camera to videotape each student's response when he encountered someone in obvious need of the services of a good Samaritan.

You're way ahead of me—student after student decided they could not stop to help the seemingly injured man because if they did they would be late for class. They knew their grade for the sermon would be negatively impacted if they didn't show up on time. Some stopped briefly to see if they could give some help—but not one of the students was late for the final exam. The real final exam happened when the professor showed each student a videotape—not of their sermon—but of their failure to be a good Samaritan like the one about whom they were prepared to preach.

After hearing about this experiment, I recounted it many times, trying to reinforce what I and so many others thought was the real lesson of this parable: *"Go and do likewise."* At the time, given my diminished spiritual vision, I thought that story would, as preachers say, "preach." And preach it I did! But as I exhorted others to be good Samaritans and help others in need, I failed to sample the true nuggets of God's grace contained in this parabolic box of chocolates.

Beyond the Façade of the Morality Gospel

Before God mercifully revealed his grace to me, I was up to my nose in the swamp of legalism. When I read the Bible I could only see those passages which seemed to proclaim the un-grace of Christ-less religion. But then came grace. God, in his mercy, started to work on me. Before the light of God's grace illuminated my heart, when I read the Good Samaritan, I reacted just like *"the expert in the law"* (Luke 10:25, 37). As a captive of religious legalism for almost 40 years, I was trained to earn God's respect and earn his rewards. My thinking was, "Tell me who I need to love, point me in the right direction, and let's get what needs to be done, done!" Like the expert in the law, I believed I could justify myself by doing precisely what I was told God wanted.

When God started to reveal the fullness of his grace to me, and invited me to receive it, I struggled to comprehend the depth of love God has for me. I struggled to trust him and believe that there really wasn't anything I could do to make him love me more. When God's grace came into my life, I had so many biblical passages to re-read and re-learn. After grace illuminated my heart, I read and studied many passages that pointed me to the grace of God, and they were incontrovertible, convincingly clear—these two, for example:

"But now apart from the law the righteousness of God has been made known, to which the Law and the Prophets testify. This righteousness is given through faith in Jesus Christ to all who believe" (Romans 3:21).

"For it is by grace you have been saved, through faith—and this is not from yourselves, it is the gift of God—not by works, so that no one can boast" (Ephesians 2:8-9).

But not all passages were crystal clear. For years an old covenant veil (2 Corinthians 3:12-18) of performance-based religion continued to at least partially obscure and diminish my freedom in Christ (Galatians 5:1).

As God mercifully continued to reveal his love to me, the parable of the Good Samaritan loomed large as one of those puzzling biblical passages. I realized that God's grace was telling me that something was not right with the traditional interpretation of the Good Samaritan I had learned, believed and passed on.

I didn't know what, but I sensed something was amiss. But each time I tried to study the parable, I continued to arrive at the same old hackneyed conclusion I had been taught. I couldn't get past seeing this parable as a moral lesson.

As it turned out, the first problem I had was with the title or name of the parable. I discovered that Jesus, the author and story-teller of the parable, may have intended that the Samaritan share twin-billing with the man who was attacked by robbers. As I continue to read and study this parable, I become more deeply convinced that Jesus chose two individuals that the religion and culture of his day perceived as nobodies to play Christ-like roles. Not only is the Good Samaritan Christ-like, so is the Good Jewish Traveler!

Before we walk through this parable we need to address a flawed religious presupposition held by many. Many are caught in the trap of believing they must perform up to a certain standard so that God will love them. According to Matthew and Luke, the greatest commandment in the law is to *"love the Lord with all your heart and with all your soul and with all your strength and with all your mind, and to love your neighbor as yourself"* (Matthew 22:37-39; Luke 10:27; see also Deuteronomy 6:5; Leviticus 19:18).

Religious legalism teaches that obedience to this greatest commandment is required of us so that God will love us in return. When it comes to the parable of the Good Samaritan, Christendom at large sees it as a command to go out and do the same as the Good Samaritan did. So Christendom enlists its subjects to go out and imitate the Samaritan. But like all other parables, this parable is ultimately not about us and what we can or must do—it's about God and what he has done and will do. For that reason the more profound spiritual lessons of this parable might be easier to taste and appreciate if we think of its core teaching as emerging from what one "loser" did for another "loser."

If the primary lesson we take away from the Good Samaritan is that we must go out and save the world by helping others, then this parable contradicts the entire gospel of Jesus Christ!

Jesus told the story of The Good Samaritan, one of his most beloved and well-known parables, as an answer to a question posed to him by a man Luke identifies as *"an expert in the law"* (Luke 10:25). The first question the expert in the law asked Jesus concerned what must be done to inherit eternal life (Luke 10:25).

Notice the emphasis—what must I *do*? What deeds must I *fulfill*? What rituals must be *performed*? What laws must be *obeyed*? What ceremonies must I *observe*?

If the primary lesson we take away from the Good Samaritan is that we must go out and save the world by helping others, then this parable contradicts the entire gospel of Jesus Christ! Any interpretation of this parable as a call to good works which will cause God to reward us with eternal life is inconsistent with the gospel:

"...For if a law had been given that could impart life, then righteousness would certainly have come by the law. But Scripture has locked up everything under the control of sin, so that what was promised, being given through faith in Jesus Christ, might be given to those who believe" (Galatians 3:21-22).

When the expert in the law wanted to know exactly what he needed to do in order to be in God's good graces, Jesus threw the question back to him, and asked him what the law said. The man quoted the great law, which says to love God and love your neighbor.

Luke comments that this religious leader wanted *"to justify himself"* (Luke 10:29)—he assumed he could demonstrate his love for God by keeping the law. He wanted to make sure he knew the precise identity of his neighbor, so that he could make sure that he loved the right person, thus fulfilling his obedience to the law.

As religious legalists always do, the expert in the law wanted to identify the exact legal requirements he needed to fulfill. So, in this same verse, the expert in the law asked his second question: *"...who is my neighbor?"*

The Good Samaritan and the Good Traveler

Responding to the expert in the law, Jesus told him a story about an unidentified, anonymous man traveling on a dangerous road from Jerusalem to Jericho who was robbed, beaten, stripped of his clothing and left for dead. The original audience who first heard this parable would have perceived this no-name, perhaps somewhat foolish traveler as a real loser. Everyone knew that the road from Jerusalem to Jericho was a notoriously dangerous stretch of road. Those up-to-no-good waited in ambush at many of the narrow turns on this hazardous road. The traveler had, for some reason, taken this road even though he must have known of the dangers.

Far from being sympathetic to the plight of this unidentified traveler, many of those who first heard this parable must have been thinking: "What was he doing on this road, alone? Didn't he know how vulnerable he was? What? Was he stupid or something?"

As Jesus skillfully continued the story, he presented two seemingly highly qualified candidates whom his audience would immediately think of as rushing to this unfortunate man's aid. Surely, thought the original audience, these two highly respected religious authorities would be a neighbor to the man in dire straits. Ironically, the presumed heroes of the story were in the same profession as the expert in the law to whom Jesus directed this parable. But alas, in Jesus' parable these two religious leaders are assigned the role of the bad guys. The expert in the law and the others who were listening to Jesus as he first gave this parable must have been just as shocked with the individuals Jesus cast in the role of bad guys as they were with the person he assigned as the good guy who helped the wounded man.

The role of the "good guy" in this parable is played by a loser—a Samaritan. To use the word "good" and "Samaritan" in the same breath was religiously scandalous to that original audience. Jews and Samaritans mutually loathed each other, as much or more than any racial or religious groups might today. Of all people, the Samaritan was the most unlikely person—the person least likely to be thought of in that society as a kind and considerate person—yet it was the Samaritan who stopped to help the man who had been left for dead.

It is easier to fulfill a list of requirements and in so doing feel you have "loved your neighbor" than it is to love Jesus, the Good Neighbor!

The Jews of that day considered themselves to be racially pure, the only true, chosen people of God, while hating and detesting their second-class Samaritan relatives. Centuries of hatred, prejudice and bigotry formed the background of Jewish-Samaritan ill will in the time of Jesus. As far as the Jewish religion was concerned, the Samaritans were heretics, half-breed losers who could not be trusted. They were unclean, unworthy outcasts—contemptible losers.

The original audience to whom Jesus gave this parable regarded Samaritans as low-life nobodies. As we have already mentioned, the traditional emphasis in this parable has been on Jesus as the Good Samaritan, and that interpretation is valid—

as far as it goes. Jesus himself was despised and rejected of men (Isaiah 53:3). But Jesus may well have assigned himself another leading role in this parable. After all, Jesus' mission to earth as one of us involved him being a battered, bruised and bloodied traveler, who knowingly walked down a dangerous road. Jesus was the traveler for whom the religious leaders of his day would not stop. He, by virtue of his earthly ministry and journey, walked down a road knowing full well the violence that awaited him. Here is our Savior suffering that we might live—dying that we might have eternal life.

Despised and Rejected by Religion

Spiritual healing and eternal life comes from the despised Carpenter from Nazareth. The real Jesus, who brings the fullness of grace (John 1:16), is still despised and rejected by religion, just as it then discredited the Samaritan. Jesus is also the traveler, the no-name who fell among thieves (Jesus continued this theme in two later parables in Luke—see 19:14 and 20:13-15). As we follow his invitation to pick up our cross and follow him (Luke 9:23), we also become fellow travelers. In his suffering he left us an example, that we should follow in his steps (1 Peter 2:21). Part of being a Christian entails walking the road from Jerusalem to Jericho, knowing full well of the danger and suffering that await us.

According to this parable, religious leaders (like the expert in the law) neglected those who were robbed and beaten and left half dead. Jesus depicted pious religious authorities as reluctant to "waste their time" serving those in need. But, as hard as it was for religious leaders to help such an unfortunate individual, which neighbor would have been more difficult for them to love: 1) the hopelessly naïve nobody traveler who, though he was robbed, beaten and left half dead, may have gotten just what he deserved or 2) the unworthy, contemptible nobody Samaritan who stopped to help the man the religious leaders passed by?

It is easier to fulfill a list of requirements and in so doing feel you have "loved your neighbor" than it is to love Jesus, the Good Neighbor! Loving Jesus means loving God's grace, the very thing that religion despises, just as it then detested the Samaritan. Loving our neighbor as ourselves means having the love of Christ, so that we love not just those we feel are deserving of our love, but those whom we may regard as disreputable nonentities.

Jesus is the despised Samaritan, the person who, in the minds of the commandment-keeping, synagogue-going audience who first heard the parable, was both highly unlikely and unqualified to render aid of any kind. It may be that Jesus also cast himself in the role of the other nobody in the parable—the no-name traveler who was beaten, bruised and battered by thieves. He came to be one of us, a fellow traveler on the many highways and byways of life, where uncertainty and danger await each and every one of us. He willingly went down the road to Jerusalem to his cross. He knew exactly what was ahead of him—yet every day of his life here on earth he continued, resolutely, to walk toward the violent end that awaited him.

Jesus' point in the parable is that religion-at-large is hostile to him, for religion sees the grace of God as silly and even dangerous. Grace is as unwelcome for Christ-less religion today as the Samaritan was to the religion of Jesus' day. The traveler willingly accepted the violence he received at the hands of all those, then and now, who reject his message of grace and peace.

Embracing His Grace

Jesus concludes the parable by saying *"Go and do likewise"* (vs. 37). If we read this verse out of the context of the lesson that precedes it, then religion and all of its rules and regulations may blind us to the grace of God. Morality based religion preaches that our primary focus must be to emulate all the actions and deeds of Jesus, and in the process misses the real significance of Jesus' teaching, in this parable and elsewhere.

As Jesus concludes this parable, telling us to *"Go and do likewise"* he is telling us to go and follow him, by allowing him to live his life in us. Jesus is not telling us to do good deeds so that God will be pleased with us on the basis of our performance. In telling us to *"Go and do likewise,"* Jesus is telling those who follow him to take up their cross and follow him. Suffer with him. Serve others, regardless of whether they seem worthy of our time and attention. This is not a parable about being a good neighbor so that we might feel good about ourselves. This is a parable inviting us to walk with Jesus, serving others in his name and suffering with him, wherever that road may lead.

Jesus also assures us that he knows what it's like to be left behind by religion, cast out of the synagogue (church), reviled and marginalized as a spiritual loser— he's walked down that road. A Christ-follower is not primarily defined by his/her own good deeds. By God's grace, a Christ-follower is known by the love of God produced in their lives by Jesus Christ, their risen Lord and Savior. A Christ-follower has received the love of God from Someone who stopped to help them in their time of need. Jesus was crucified as an enemy of religion, judged to be less worthy of life than a notorious criminal and condemned to torture and death as a nobody:

"The high priest carries the blood of animals into the Most Holy Place as a sin offering, but the bodies are burned outside the camp. And so Jesus also suffered outside the city gate to make the people holy through his own blood. Let us, then, go to him outside the camp, bearing the disgrace he bore" (Hebrews 13:11-13).

Incredible as it may seem, Jesus shows mercy not only to those who are lost and know that they are lost—he is filled with compassion for all of the highbrow religious folks who are so proud of their religious accomplishments and have no idea they are lost. I know that Jesus is filled with compassion for self-righteous, pride-filled, arrogant spiritual hypocrites. But for his grace, as for legalistic righteousness, I would still be trying to be faultless (Philippians 3:6). But for God's grace, I would still be busy filling my spiritual trophy case.

CHAPTER 5

HE BECOMES ONE OF THE FLOCK

"Very truly I tell you Pharisees, anyone who does not enter the sheep pen by the gate, but climbs in by some other way, is a thief and a robber. The one who enters by the gate is the shepherd of the sheep. The gatekeeper opens the gate for him, and the sheep listen to his voice. He calls his own sheep by name and leads them out. When he has brought out all his own, he goes on ahead of them, and his sheep follow him because they know his voice. But they will never follow a stranger; in fact, they will run away from him because they do not recognize a stranger's voice." Jesus used this figure of speech, but the Pharisees did not understand what he was telling them.

Therefore Jesus said again, "Very truly I tell you, I am the gate for the sheep. All who have come before me are thieves and robbers, but the sheep have not listened to them. I am the gate; whoever enters through me will be saved. They will come in and go out, and find pasture. The thief comes only to steal and kill and destroy; I have come that they may have life, and have it to the full.

I am the good shepherd. The good shepherd lays down his life for the sheep. The hired hand is not the shepherd and does not own the sheep. So when he sees the wolf coming, he abandons the sheep and runs away. Then the wolf attacks the flock and scatters it. The man runs away because he is a hired hand and cares nothing for the sheep.

I am the good shepherd; I know my sheep and my sheep know me—just as the Father knows me and I know the Father—and I lay down my life for the sheep. I have other sheep that are not of this sheep pen. I must bring them also. They too will listen to my voice, and there shall be one flock and one shepherd. The reason my Father loves me is that I lay down my life—only to take it up again. No one takes it from me, but I lay it down of my own accord. I have authority to lay it down and authority to take it up again. This command I received from my Father."—John 10:1-18

> There was a man who dwelt in the east centuries ago,
> Now I cannot look at a sheep or a sparrow,
> A lily or a cornfield, a raven or a sunset,
> A vineyard or a mountain, without thinking of him.
> —G.K. Chesterton

Darkness was giving way to dawn as he finished his hike to the top of a hill. As he prayed during this time of solitude, rays of sunshine induced the hillside on the other side of the valley to display magnificent shades and hues of color not seen at other times of the day. When the light of a new day started to reach the valley below, shepherds sleeping alongside their flock started to stir.

Ending his time of prayer, his gaze fell on the shepherds rising from their blankets, and the solitary man's thoughts focused on his own human sheep. He was a shepherd as well—he loved his flock of *homo sapiens*. He loved human sheep so much that he had come from eternity, so that he could become one of them. Just as the shepherds in the valley below were starting another day of tending to their flocks, it was time for him to begin another day, as well. He started to walk back to the campsite where some of his sheep, his disciples, were sleeping. It was time to wake them up and prepare their breakfast.

"I am the good shepherd; I know my sheep and my sheep know me—just as the Father knows me and I know the Father—and I lay down my life for the sheep" (John 10:14-15).

The Great I AM Who Became One of His Sheep

Centuries of traditions and images of Jesus have filled our minds and inform us how to think of him. When we hear about Jesus being our shepherd we often think of sweet Jesus, perhaps holding a sheep in his arms. We think of Jesus, as pictured in Psalm 23 ("The Lord is My Shepherd"), walking with us beside still waters. Well intentioned attempts to depict the reality of Jesus have effectively tamed and domesticated him for the religious market.

For many professing Christians, the idea of Jesus as our Good Shepherd conjures up idyllic, sentimental thoughts of Jesus—the Good Shepherd, wearing a sparkling white robe, like an advertisement for a modern day detergent or fabric softener—cradling a little lamb whose fleece is white as snow. But the reality of Jesus as our "Good" Shepherd and of Jesus becoming one of his own sheep is far from a romantic, sanitized Sunday school lesson.

It's often called a parable, but as with many of Jesus' teachings recorded in the Gospel of John, the Good Shepherd is really more of an extended metaphor. Parable or metaphor, the Good Shepherd is one of the great I AM statements in the Gospel of John—assertions that provide a unique insight and perspective into the nature of Jesus, the God-man, and his mission and identity:

- I AM the bread of life (John 6:35).
- I AM the light of the world (John 8:12; 9:5).
- I AM the gate for the sheep (John 10:7).
- I AM the good shepherd (John 10:11,14).
- I AM the resurrection and the life (John 11:25).
- I AM the way and the truth and the life (John 14:6).
- I AM the true vine (John 15:1).

By the time of Jesus, the once honorable and highly esteemed profession of shepherding had taken an incredible nosedive. The book of Genesis tells us that the great patriarchs Abraham, Isaac and Jacob were all shepherds. Genesis begins the story of mankind by praising Abel, who *"kept flocks"* (Genesis 4:2), as the good son of Adam and Eve. Moses, another revered Hebrew patriarch, was tending sheep when the great I AM appeared to him (Exodus 3:1-14).

Over time, the literal occupation of shepherding seems to have become less prestigious in the culture of Israel. Taking care of the sheep was considered to be the least honorable job in David's family, for he, as the youngest and therefore least regarded of Jesse's sons, was assigned to tend the sheep (1 Samuel 16:11). Still, the prophets of God continued to use the metaphor of shepherds in context with both civil and religious leaders. While herding sheep was once regarded as a respectable profession, when Jesus was born shepherds were regarded with skepticism and scorn.

By identifying himself as the Good Shepherd, Jesus was clearly saying that he alone was the good spiritual shepherd humanity had never before experienced (see the Messianic promise in Jeremiah 23:1-4). This bold assertion that

> **Religion has tamed and domesticated Jesus so that he conforms to religious ideals.**

he was the Good Shepherd was a bold proclamation of his deity, and did little to endear him to the spiritual professionals of his day. Jesus deliberately distanced himself from religious professionals who were charter members of the rules, regulations, rituals and ceremonies society. Instead, Jesus identified with people who had miserably failed to meet the membership criteria for inclusion in polite, church-going society. He identified with "losers" so much that he became one!

Jesus is the Good Shepherd—as opposed to the accepted stereotype of spiritual shepherds. Jesus is the Good Shepherd unlike religious shepherds who fleece the flock rather than serve it. Jesus continually dismayed the religious establishment of his day (and truth be known, many religious professionals today!) because he did not act like they expected him to act. He did not say the things they expected to hear. He openly questioned and violated the religious sacred cows of his day.

The heroes of Jesus' teachings and his parables were despised Samaritans and shepherds, rather than pompous, pious, ceremony-observing, rules-happy Pharisees. Jesus focused his attention and ministry on lepers and prostitutes rather than on the worldly wisdom and righteousness of respected priests and teachers of the law. Jesus reached out to "unimportant" children and women.

Shepherds in the First Century

Shepherding was one of the major occupations in first-century Palestine. Shepherds were known as rugged, rough-and-tumble, out-of-doors individuals who worked in remote areas, confronting danger from wild animals and would-be thieves. When the disciples, and later the original readers of the Gospel of John, heard Jesus describe himself as a "Good" Shepherd they would have thought of a shepherd with a weather-beaten face, dressed in homespun clothing, and smelling like...sheep!

Jesus may have deliberately identified himself with a profession that didn't have the best reputation—he did a similar thing with the parable of the Good Samaritan. As we discussed in Chapter Four, in the first-century religious world of the Jews, all Samaritans were bad—none of them were considered as having any religious worth—they were all seen as spiritually undeserving.

The religious community was outraged that Jesus' followers accepted him as a rabbi and teacher though his teaching was not based on respectable, well educated, long-since-deceased religious theologians and authorities—like their own. Instead of identifying his teaching with religious authorities, Jesus compared himself to a Samaritan, someone whose profession demanded little, if any, education. On top of all that, Jesus said that he had come to serve, rather than to be served (Matthew 20:28). The religious establishment's disgust for Jesus had to intensify when he identified his spiritual vocation with the disreputable profession of shepherding.

Shepherds who watched over their sheep were nomads. As our Good Shepherd Jesus said, *"Foxes have dens and birds have nests, but the Son of Man has no place to lay his head"* (Matthew 8:20). Life was hard for shepherds—theirs was not a high-paying profession. They suffered from exposure to the elements. They didn't sleep in a warm home or shelter.

THE HEROES of JESUS' TEACHING AND his PARABLES WERE despised SAMARITANS AND shepHERds, RATHER THAN pompous, pious, CEREMONY-observiNG, RULES-HAppy PHARisEES.

Shepherds were distrusted—first-century society felt that they could not be relied on to provide honest eyewitness testimony. If a similar prejudice existed in North America today, shepherds would automatically be excused from jury service. Ironically, when the Chief Shepherd of our souls came to this earth to be a sheep, to be one of us, he first appeared to shepherds. Shepherds, of all people, were the first witnesses to his earthly life!

Had we been asked to write the script for Jesus' first appearance, we might have devised a plan for respected religious leaders—perhaps the Pope and the Archbishop of Canterbury—to be in attendance at his birth. But Jesus wasn't born in any cathedral or sanctuary surrounded by stained glass.

Jesus was born far from the front doors of any cathedral—far from any mega-church—far from the holy ground of any temple. The place where Jesus was born had more in common with places today where homeless people fill shopping carts with redeemable containers and poor day laborers wait for someone to hire them.

Jesus describes himself in the book of Revelation as knock, knock, knocking on the door of established and respected buildings which house congregations—he is outside, looking in (Revelation 3:20). He was no stranger to being on the outside, looking in—those were the circumstances of his birth, when no room was found for Joseph, Mary and the soon-to-be-born Jesus at the inn at Bethlehem (Luke 2:7) Jesus was born with animals in attendance, with shepherds among the first witnesses. Homeless people without an address and undocumented, illegal workers aren't asked to serve on juries today either, are they?

The Bible speaks of three kinds of shepherds: 1) *hired hands,* 2) *bad shepherds* and 3) *good shepherds.*

Hired hands are in it for the money. They have no stake in the future of the flock. Hired hands do the bare minimum, because the sheep are not their own.

Bad shepherds drive the sheep rather than lead them. Bad shepherds often feel they are strong leaders when they push and beat and abuse the sheep. Bad shepherds have a selfish stake in the future of the sheep they "serve." They are only interested in the personal benefits they can derive from the sheep. When hired hands and bad shepherds lead/rule over/control and dominate the sheep, the sheep do not thrive—they barely survive.

The *good shepherd* gently leads the sheep. He leads them in such a way that any enemy—human or animal—must get through the shepherd first before it can ravage the flock. Good shepherds lay down their lives for their sheep, rather than the other way around. Good shepherds call the sheep by name, and the sheep know the shepherd's voice. Good shepherds willingly serve the sheep, rather than seeing them as just another chore or task to be fulfilled.

What Makes Jesus a "Good" Shepherd?

1) Jesus is the Good Shepherd because he provides protection for his sheep in a sheep pen. The first-century sheep pen was more like a rough stone or mud structure—or a cave in the hills—than it was a fenced-in corral. The sheep pen had only one opening through which the sheep, after a day of grazing, would enter for the night, so that they could be protected from thieves, robbers and predatory animals. As the sheep entered through the gate the shepherd would inspect each one individually—the shepherd would treat and anoint scratched or wounded sheep—the shepherd would provide water for thirsty sheep. Then once all the sheep passed into the sheep pen, the shepherd laid down his life—placing his body in the opening of the pen, sleeping between his sheep and enemies who might harm them. The shepherd personally became the gate (John 10:7).

2) Jesus is the Good Shepherd because he heals and feeds and waters his sheep. Jesus is genuinely concerned for our welfare—whereas some who pretend to be spiritual shepherds exploit the sheep, making merchandise of them through trickery and deception or abuse. Jesus not only feeds and provides for the physical needs of his sheep, but far more than that, he provides spiritual life. The Good

Shepherd is good, not just morally good, but good in the ultimate sense—the Good Shepherd personifies and defines *Good* because he is God. In the sixth chapter of the Gospel of John we read that Jesus is the true bread of life and in the seventh chapter of the Gospel of John he identifies himself as the life-giving stream of living water.

As John 10:10 says, the Good Shepherd came so that we might have life. He came to give us eternal life, life of the age to come. He came that we might live in him and he in us, now and forevermore, because he lays down his life for us.

WHEN HIRED HANDS AND BAD SHEPHERDS LEAD/RULE OVER/ CONTROL AND DOMINATE THE SHEEP, THE SHEEP DO NOT THRIVE— THEY BARELY SURVIVE.

Jesus is the Good Shepherd not simply because he dies instead of his sheep. His sacrificial death for us is only part of the story of who and what he is, and how he is truly our Good Shepherd. While other biblical references to Jesus as the Lamb of God concern his voluntary work in taking the consequences of the flock's sins, the Good Shepherd describes himself as laying down his life and then taking it back again.

Jesus, our Good Shepherd, didn't merely allow himself to be killed—he proactively and voluntarily gave his life and then, as he says in John 10:17, "*I lay down my life—only to take it up again.*" Any human being can voluntarily die for someone else or for a cause—but only God in the flesh could voluntarily die as a supreme expression of divine love and then resume that life, taking "*it up again.*"

He was not simply a passive victim of his enemies,

but he was an active participant in reconciling all humanity, and beyond that, all creation to himself.

"For God was pleased to have all his fullness dwell in him, and through him to reconcile to himself all things, whether things on earth or things in heaven, by making peace through his blood, shed on the cross."
—Colossians 1:19-20

3) Jesus is the Good Shepherd because he loves everyone—the entire world. Jesus has, as verse 16 says, other sheep that are not of any particular sheep pen. Jesus is not leading a closed door religious commune or country club. All are welcome in the body of Christ—everyone can be part of his flock. Jesus has no favorites—he does not discriminate. He is above the boundaries and limitations religion sets for its membership. He is the Good Shepherd because, as strange as it might seem to some, Jesus doesn't have a favorite church or religion.

4) Jesus is the Good Shepherd because he knows his sheep and they know him. Hired hands and "bad" shepherds do not take the time Jesus does to know his sheep, allowing his sheep to come to know him. Jesus did not remain in heaven, detached, distant and immune from the hardships and dangers facing his flock. Jesus, the Good Shepherd, descended into our world, becoming one of us—knowing us by becoming one of us—and allowing us to know him. We know his voice because of his willingness to leave the splendor and eternity of heaven, and while remaining divine, also becoming human—experiencing firsthand what it's like to be a *homo sapien* sheep.

In Christ, our relationship with our Good Shepherd is like the harmonious divine relationship he has with the Father. In Christ, we are one with and in our Good Shepherd just as God—Father, Son and Holy Spirit—is one. The Triune Godhead is one in purpose, one in attitude and outlook and one in perfect harmony—and the product of that harmony is the peace of God. We can know and experience that peace because we know Jesus, the Good Shepherd, and he knows us. We know him and he knows us in a far greater way than merely knowing *about* him, or him knowing *about* us.

We don't merely have cognitive knowledge or awareness of Jesus—nor is his knowing us limited to simple information. We don't know Jesus by researching him on the Internet. We don't know him by knowing facts about his earthly life. We do not know him in a detached, arms-length way. He invites us to know him, the Good Shepherd, intimately—and in that relationship we come to trust and rely on the Good Shepherd because of his love for us. He loved us first (1 John 4:19) and then, because of his expression of love, we are able to respond to his love and love him back.

When Adam and Eve were first created, the Creator, the very divine Person who is our Good Shepherd, told them they would become one flesh. They would share the most sacred and intimate of all human relationships—they would, through sexual intimacy, share the highest expression of human love, and unite because of their commitment to each other.

The Good Shepherd, in his incarnation, as he came to us, came to be one of us and one with us. He came so that we might come to know him. His love for each of us is such that he relentlessly expresses his love for us—he never stops reaching out to us with his love. He invites us—he proposes to us—that we would become one in him and with him—so that we unite with him, we live a life in union with Christ. Jesus is therefore not just any shepherd, but he is truly the Good Shepherd.

The Games Losers Play

Psalm 23 (The Lord is My Shepherd) and John 10 both identify you and me as sheep. God's use of the sheep metaphor yields many insights into the nature of our relationship with God. Sheep have no weapons. They have no fangs or claws. They have no shell for protection. They are near-sighted and are not blessed with keen hearing. They are slow moving, with little strength or stamina, and their poor sense of direction is legendary. Sheep are easily terrified and predisposed to wander away from the flock. God compares us to sheep because we humans are not as spiritually tough, independent and intelligent as we would like to think. Sheep need constant attention. We need the Good Shepherd.

Just as sheep cannot sleep unless they trust the shepherd who gives them peace and rest from predators, Jesus offers us rest in him (Matthew 11:28-30). The relationship between a shepherd and his flock is unique, unlike any other human-animal relationship. The one attribute which is perhaps best known about sheep is that they are dumb and helpless. Jesus even gave us a parable about dumb sheep getting lost.

Luke 15:4-7 is one of three parables, all grouped together, that speak of God's love for the least, the lost and the last. Some Bible translations point out the continuity in these three parables in Luke 15 by calling them the parable of the lost sheep (vs.

3-7), the parable of the lost coin (vs. 8-10) and the parable of the lost son (vs. 11-32). But it is also important to keep in mind the immediate audience to whom Jesus directed these three parables.

The first two verses of Luke 15 tell us that the religious leaders were upset that Jesus welcomed and ate meals with sinners. Eating with another person was considered a sign of acceptance, common ground and fellowship in that culture. These religious leaders who were upset that Jesus was embracing "sinners" were saying, in essence, that Jesus himself was a "bad" shepherd, because he hung out with "bad" people. As happens so often in Jesus' teaching, he turned the tables on these spiritual know-it-alls.

> **HE is THE Good ShEphErd bEcaUSE, aS STRangE aS iT MighT SEEM TO SOME, JESUS doESN'T havE a favoriTE chURch OR RELigioN.**

Jesus immediately placed the religious leaders on the defensive by using the well-known metaphor of shepherding to discuss spiritual leadership and service. These religious leaders were upset that he was spending time with spiritual failures and losers, so Jesus reasoned, "Fine, let's talk about losers and why they are lost and how they can be rescued."

Jesus begins the parable, *"Suppose one of you has a hundred sheep and loses one of them"* (Luke 15:4). From the very beginning Jesus makes it clear that the blame for losing this spiritual sheep was at the door of these shepherds.

Then Jesus drops the second bombshell. He says, *"Doesn't he leave the ninety-nine in the open country and go after the lost sheep until he finds it?"*

(Luke 15:4). One of the major teaching points in the parable of the lost sheep is that the truly good shepherd, upon realizing that one of his flock of 100 sheep was lost, leaves the other 99, and uses all his available resources to rescue the one sheep.

The worth that Jesus attached to one lost sheep seemed ludicrous to religious leaders who didn't like Jesus spending time with people who weren't dues-paying members of their holiness societies. These religious leaders, who seemed to be spiritual legends in their own eyes, felt that shepherds, whether of the dirty and despised physical variety, or of the respected religious persuasion, such as themselves, did not leave 99 percent of the flock to recover one.

Jesus was suggesting that a shepherd would make what seemed to be an obviously flawed business decision by leaving 99 percent of the flock to recover one. He was also suggesting that this event took place in *"open country"* where it would be suicidal to leave the 99 percent.

In these religious leaders' minds Jesus had said many "stupid" things so far—but this one took the cake. It had to rank as one of the most illogical and off-the-wall things this untrained so-called rabbi had ever said!

These religious scholars had all taken *Basic Spiritual Shepherding 101*, where they learned that the primary duty of shepherding was to take care of the healthy, promising sheep, and never, ever expend so much time and resources on the needy few that you, as a shepherd, might risk losing the majority of the flock.

But Jesus hadn't taken that class—he had bypassed (much to the religious leaders' disapproval) their seminaries and their indoctrination.

His teaching was all about going after the least, the lost and the last.

Though the parable was a not-so-thinly-veiled rebuke of these religious leaders, Jesus was not giving this parable to tell them (or us) how to be a successful religious shepherd. The parable is all about God's grace. After all, the Good Shepherd would be the only shepherd who could ever dare to take the extreme risks Jesus described this shepherd as taking.

God's grace doesn't make sense. It isn't practical. It means that God puts himself out there, almost inviting people to take advantage of his good graces.

But the real emphasis of the parable is the incredible love of God which often, to the human mind, doesn't seem to add up. From our human perspective and judgment, God's grace simply does not compute.

God's grace doesn't make sense. It isn't practical. It means that God puts himself out there, almost inviting people to take advantage of his good graces. And that's exactly what he does!

God doesn't play by religious rules. He's not into percentages. He doesn't play religious numbers games. Our relationship with him is not based on keeping score. God's grace doesn't make human sense—neither does it make sense for the Good Shepherd to leave 99 percent who have promise of providing a positive financial return, and go after one who can never repay him. Church leaders think, "How in the world would we pay the bills if we did such a thing?" Perhaps the "bigger is better" criterion of success generally accepted within the religious world today ought to give us pause for thought.

Peace on Earth

Immediately following the angel's announcement of the birth of Jesus to the shepherds who were keeping watch over their flocks in the hills just outside of Bethlehem, a heavenly choir punctuated the announcement with a proclamation in the form of an anthem:

"Glory to God in the highest heaven, and on earth peace to those on whom his favor rests" (Luke 2:14).

A paradoxical statement, if ever there was one! There was no peace in Bethlehem then, or for that matter, now. The world to which Jesus was born groaned under brutal Roman oppression—the so-called *Pax Romana*. Roman peace was achieved through intimidation, military power, threats, abuse, torture and slavery (experts say some 20-30 percent of the population under Roman domination were enslaved). The people of Judea were subjected to ruthless taxation which impoverished them. And this choir was singing *"peace on earth."* They obviously didn't live anywhere near Bethlehem!

But the anthem didn't proclaim that the entire world was at peace. The anthem didn't proclaim that the entire world would soon be at peace. The anthem simply proclaimed that Peace had arrived, in the person of the Good Shepherd, Jesus Christ. The angel told the shepherds the sign of the coming of Peace to the town of David (Bethlehem) would be *"a baby wrapped in cloths and lying in a manger"* (Luke 2:12).

It was another paradoxical sign that what God does often defies human convention and logic. Babies, along with shepherds, were among the powerless, helpless and desperately-in-need people generally regarded as worthless and given little, if any, respect in that culture. A baby was bringing peace. A baby, in a feeding trough, was Christ the Lord—the Prince of peace.

He brought peace to all mankind because he embodied the favor and the grace of God. He offers you and me, his sheep, that same rest, that same favor and that same grace. We are the sheep of his pasture—he is the Shepherd and Overseer of our souls (1 Peter 2:25).

CHAPTER 6

UNCIRCULATED, MINT CONDITION GRACE?

"Again, it will be like a man going on a journey, who called his servants and entrusted his wealth to them. To one he gave five bags of gold, to another two bags, and to another one bag, each according to his ability. Then he went on his journey.

The man who had received five bags of gold went at once and put his money to work and gained five bags more.

So also, the one with two bags of gold gained two more. But the man who had received one bag went off, dug a hole in the ground and hid his master's money.

After a long time the master of those servants returned and settled accounts with them. The man who had received five bags of gold brought the other five. 'Master,' he said, 'you entrusted me with five bags of gold. See, I have gained five more.'

His master replied, 'Well done, good and faithful servant! You have been faithful with a few things; I will put you in charge of many things. Come and share your master's happiness!'

The man with two bags of gold also came. 'Master,' he said, 'you entrusted me with two bags of gold; see, I have gained two more.'

His master replied, 'Well done, good and faithful servant! You have been faithful with a few things; I will put you in charge of many things. Come and share your master's happiness!

Then the man who had received one bag of gold came. 'Master,' he said, 'I knew that you are a hard man, harvesting where you have not sown and gathering where you have not scattered seed. So I was afraid and went out and hid your gold in the ground. See, here is what belongs to you.'

His master replied, 'You wicked, lazy servant! So you knew that I harvest where I have not sown and gather where I have not scattered seed? Well then, you should have put my money on deposit with the bankers, so that when I returned I would have received it back with interest.

So take the bag of gold from him and give it to the one who has ten bags. For whoever has will be given more, and they will have an abundance. Whoever does not have, even what they have will be taken from them. And throw that worthless servant outside, into the darkness, where there will be weeping and gnashing of teeth.'—Matthew 25:14-30.

The parable of the talents, as the parable we are considering in this chapter is traditionally titled, is the second of three parables in Matthew 25. The first bookend surrounding this parable about, as more recent translations have it, bags of gold, is the parable of the bridesmaids

(Matthew 25:1-13)—centered around the self-inflicted judgment experienced by five foolish bridesmaids who don't have enough lamp oil for their middle-of-the-night journey to meet the bridegroom. The parable of the bridesmaids has historically been a happy hunting-ground for preachers who place an interpretation which serves the needs of institutionalized religion on the differences between the "wise" and the "foolish" bridesmaids (if you haven't heard one of these harangues, rest assured that they all are based on the religious performance of the bridesmaids). Such diatribes often give precise definitions for what the oil, the lamps, sleep and the midnight hour supposedly represent.

The other bookend surrounding the parable of the bags of gold is the parable of the judgment (Matthew 25:31-46), about a shepherd/king who separates sheep and goats inter-mingled in his flock. An ultimate division of sheep and goats in a shepherd's flock, mixed together up until that point, was a common feature of Palestinian flocks. It was difficult, superficially, to distinguish sheep and goats, and Jesus plays on that common occurrence in this parable. A similar lesson is drawn in the parable of the weeds (Matthew 13:24-30), another kingdom parable, when we see that the owner of a wheat field deliberately allowed both wheat and weeds to grow together until the harvest. Poisonous darnel was well known to Palestinian farmers for its close resemblance, particularly in the early stages of growth, to bearded wheat.

In the parable of the judgment the shepherd/king calls attention to the authentic human sheep who serve *"the least of these brothers and sisters of* mine" (Matthew 25:40), apparently without giving their service a second thought. The shepherd/king commends those who, as his sheep, serve others because of their "sheep nature"—they take little notice of their service to others. When we read the "rest of the story" in the New Testament we realize that Jesus' sheep serve others as a way of life because they have been transformed by Christ (Romans 6:4; 2 Corinthians 5:17; Galatians 2:20).

The goats choose to live by the sword of legalism and therefore subject themselves to a legalistic judgment.

The goats, on the other hand, are so conscious of their good deeds (feverishly racking up spiritual brownie points they assume they will cash in on judgment day) that they can't remember a time when they were not performing good deeds.

The parable reveals that the basis of judgment is what Christ has done, is doing and will do in the lives of his sheep, rather than goat-like performance exhibited in those who are primarily motivated and driven by religious ideals.

This parable of judgment concludes with the judgment chosen by those who believe their own deeds gain them superior spiritual standing, as opposed to the blessings given to those who realize that they, apart from Jesus, have nothing to offer. The goats choose to live by the sword of legalism and therefore subject themselves to a legalistic judgment. The goats choose their judgment—they are self-cursed.

As with the parable of the bridesmaids, the first parabolic bookend to the parable of the bags of gold, the parable of the judgment is considered great fodder for hell-fire-and-brimstone preachers who depict God as sending people into the eternal torment of hell-fire because they failed to measure up to religious standards.

Talents or Bags of Gold?

As we turn our attention to a parable that has been historically labeled as the parable of the talents we first need to realize that this parable uses the term "talent" as a monetary reference to help illustrate its primary point. However, the world "talent" has taken on far more than financial definition. Dictionaries trace the origin of the contemporary definition of the word "talent" as a natural or supernatural gift back to this parable. Along with many other translations of the Bible, The New International Version (NIV) I read and studied for more than twenty years used the word "talent." However, the most recent version of the NIV I am now using (2011) simply says *"bag(s) of gold."*

"Bag(s) of gold" is a far better translation than "talent" because it avoids an emphasis on human traits and aptitudes which can cause us to miss the point of this parable. In addition, *"bag(s) of gold,"* because it is far less precise in measuring a specific monetary value, avoids calling attention to a conversion of the amount of money represented by a "talent" then into a precise equivalent today.

So what's the problem with taking the time to find out what ten thousand talents or ten thousand bags of gold are worth, in today's money? In Chapter Three we examined another parable which uses money as a means of conveying a profound spiritual truth, the unforgiving servant of Matthew

18:21-35. Having been miraculously forgiven of a debt of ten thousand bags of gold by his king, the unforgiving servant is unable or unwilling to pass on similar forgiveness of a small fraction owed to him by one of his fellow-servants.

The precise amount owed by the unforgiving servant is immaterial. We can bog down, and potentially miss the point by fixating on a specific amount the servant owed. He owed more than he could ever repay—as we postulated in Chapter Three, probably something on the order of a debt that would have taken him 5,000 lifetimes to repay.

In this parable in Matthew 25, three servants are given bags of gold. Without making too much of what the amount might be today, the most informed estimates I have seen would place the gift of five bags of gold to the first servant as somewhere in the neighborhood of $3.75 million U.S. dollars today. The second servant was given two bags—perhaps an amount equal to about $1.5 million U.S. dollars. And finally, the third servant was given one bag—something like $750,000.

The master didn't give these servants merely a small tip or an allowance—they received an incredible amount of money. One, two or five bags of gold was not then, nor is it today, chump change. As we immerse ourselves in the teaching of this parable, we should consider how these three servants must have felt. Servants (slaves) at that time earned minimal wages, and while they could earn bonuses it was unheard of for a slave to ever accumulate enough personal capital to invest.

At the same time, it was not uncommon at that time for masters taking long trips to entrust financial assets to their slaves. When that happened, a servant (slave) physically experienced what Paul described spiritually as *"the incomparable riches of his grace"* (see Ephesians 2:7). The master *"entrusted his wealth"* (Matthew 25:14) to his servants. The servants found themselves in uncharted territory—they had never before been given such an incredible gift. They were well aware that they had been given what they could never earn!

Not only is such lavish trust uncharted territory in terms of physical economics, it completely flies in the face of established and accepted religious practice. Christ-less religion is a system of prescribed behavior which insists that human performance earns divine reward. Authentic Christianity teaches that God's favor is given and entrusted to those who respond to him with trust and faith—who realize that they are incapable of earning favor from him on the basis of their performance.

"Come, all you who are thirsty, come to the waters; and you who have no money, come, buy and eat! Come, buy wine and milk without money and without cost. Why spend money on what is not bread, and your labor on what does not satisfy? Listen, listen to me, and eat what is good, and you will delight in the richest of fare" (Isaiah 55:1-2).

The three servants had received a lavish amount of grace—grace they could never earn. What did the master want them to do?

Grace in Action

The first two servants doubled the master's gift. The parable doesn't provide details of how they gained such a return, nor does it give us any hint that the master was the least bit interested in the details about how his gift had increased. That detail, like the precise amount of the monetary gift, appears to be immaterial to the story. The parable doesn't say whether the two servants invested in the race track or real estate, banking or bootlegging or whether their investment strategies were legal or illegal. It just says that they doubled the gift. They built on the trust they had been shown, because they were willing to risk what they had been given.

God is no micro-manager, constantly looking over our shoulders, prodding us to do more and do better. He entrusts us with his grace and takes a long journey.

When the master returned, the third servant could only present him with his unsullied, pristine, unused bag of gold. Given the master's response in Matthew 25:26 ("*You wicked, lazy servant*"), we can safely assume that God is not impressed by *uncirculated, mint condition grace*! It would seem that the master would have preferred that this servant lost the entire bag of gold trying something rather than risking nothing.

The third servant buried grace like a dead corpse. It's an insult to God's vibrant grace to hide it, bury it or hoard it! Attempting to hoard the gift of God is spiritual death. Humanly, it may seem that the third servant took the safe and secure path, safeguarding God's grace. "After all," says human reason, "at least he didn't lose God's grace!"

The master had entrusted his wealth so that these three fund managers of his grace could turn the wealth loose. He wasn't concerned how much "money" they made or lost—he wanted the riches of his grace circulated. He called these two servants "good and faithful" because they were willing to spend the grace he had so freely given them.

The third servant operated out of fear (by his own admission), rather than faith. He said, when his master asked him why he had buried the bag of gold, *"I was afraid and went out and hid your gold in the ground"* (Matthew 25:25).

The third servant operated out of a religious paradigm. He feared God as a *"hard man"* (Matthew 25:24). He believed the lie that he could only please the master on the basis of his performance, and he didn't trust his own abilities to perform up to such a level. The third servant, a slave of religion, didn't really believe that his master trusted him.

> THE THIRD SERVANT BURIED GRACE LIKE A DEAD CORPSE. IT'S AN INSULT TO GOD'S VIBRANT GRACE TO HIDE IT, BURY IT OR HOARD IT!

What is the focus of this parable? Along with the first parable in Matthew 25, it is a parable describing what the kingdom of heaven is like. Careful readers of Matthew's Gospel recognize the familiar, formulaic introduction of Matthew 25:1 *"the kingdom of heaven will be like..."*

When Jesus followed that parable with this parable of the bags of gold he introduced it with *"Again, it will be like..."* (Matthew 25:14). This parable, like all kingdom parables, is devoted to helping us understand the nature of the relationship God offers to us. Will we trust our own abilities or will we trust God's grace? Will we trust religious methodologies or will we trust in Christ to do for us what we can never do for ourselves?

The grace that the master entrusted to these

three servants was given to them "up front." Grace was given without stipulation or qualification. There is no mention that the master insisted they sign a pledge or a contract. They were not asked to sign a membership covenant guaranteeing faithful attendance "at church" every week and 10% tithing as a condition of the master's grace. No signatures were necessary—grace is God's lavish, undeserved trust.

What does the master want in return? Is he looking for us to earn the grace we have been given? No, that's impossible—these servants could never have earned the amount given to them. What does God want "for" his grace? He wants trust—he yearns for relationship.

This parable is often preached at "stewardship" drives, when church members are reminded of their responsibility to donate (or is it more like being guilted into giving?). The passage is thus abused, turning divine grace into human religious performance! The idea that we must work and work and work and then wait, on pins and needles, for the final judgment of God, hoping that he will say "well done," violates and corrupts the gospel of Jesus Christ!

The third servant completely misunderstood his master. He didn't perceive his master as loving and generous, but unforgiving and vindictive. The third servant was like many within Christendom today who perceive God as a harsh and stern taskmaster. The third servant accused his master of "harvesting where you have not sown" (vs. 24) when, in fact, the master had given him the bag of gold in the first place! Many who are enslaved to Christ-less religion today fear God in a similar way as the third servant feared his master. The master has no words of praise for the third servant, but within the context of what the servant didn't do with the one bag of gold he was given, calls the servant *wicked* and *lazy* (vs. 26) and *worthless* (vs. 30).

The master gave the bag(s) of gold—the servants did not earn or deserve them. The bag(s) were a gift, a sacred deposit of God's very own grace, which cannot be earned by human effort. The master did not give equally. The master did not give each of the three servants the same "measure" of his grace. They all received his grace—they all received his generosity—but in different "amounts" or degrees.

The master expected the gifts he gave to be used. He intended for the bags of gold he gave to be shared, circulated, broadcast and distributed. This parable comes back to the master's generosity and his determination to share what was his to begin with.

The servants weren't expected to produce more gold—likewise we are not expected to generate more grace, which is of course humanly impossible. No human can manufacture such a priceless and precious spiritual gift. The servants were (and are) simply asked to share his grace, because God's grace is dynamic—it grows as it is shared and passed on. The master merely asked that his servants become channels, conduits and vehicles of his grace. The master didn't want his grace returned (as the third servant thought)—he wanted it to be shared!

The message of grace is that we are all held in God's eternal embrace of love through the faithfulness of Jesus Christ. We are already forgiven. We are already saved. We are already invited to his eternal banquet. We are already infinitely and eternally loved. Because of Jesus, God already says *"well done"* to those who accept and trust him. Nothing can separate us from the love of God, says Paul in Romans 8:39.

The parable of the bags of gold (talents) is often abused by performance-based religion, as it is offered as an example of how humans might be saved by grace, but rewarded for works. When that interpretation is preached, the emphasis is often on *"well done"* as if that phrase directly connects our efforts with the receipt of God's grace.

But such an interpretation completely misses the point of both the parable and the gospel! The parable does not specifically say that either one of the two servants whose gifts doubled did so as a result of their own diligent efforts. They simply told the master that they had gained the same number of bags of gold as he had given them.

How had they gained those bags of gold? Well, we get a clue from the person who buried their talent in the ground. God's gifts are not meant to be buried. We are not the end user of God's gifts.

The third servant operated out of fear, and he received the fear he had chosen. Fear is its own judgment. John tells us that perfect love drives out fear (1 John 4:18). Life in Christ is not a life of fear, but a relationship of trust and joy. The master didn't have to pronounce judgment on the third servant—he had sentenced himself. God is not pronouncing a judgment—he is merely describing it.

The third servant was proud he had accounted for every penny he was given. The false spiritual security in which the third servant luxuriated—his possession of *uncirculated, mint condition grace*—sentenced him to a living hell. When the third servant buried the grace he was given, he dug his own spiritual grave.

God's grace cannot be bottled up and stored away in a "safe" place so that we and we alone may enjoy and profit from it. God's grace is dynamic—it defies anyone or any group who will try to hoard it for themselves. By virtue of accepting God's grace we realize that God will use us as an instrument to freely distribute his grace. In that way, the grace God gives us is multiplied. In God's grace economy, his grace is paid forward, distributed and multiplied. We grow in God's grace as we yield our lives as vehicles of his grace.

We will thus hear the praise *"well done"* from our master when we embrace his love, when we unconditionally accept his grace—when we give up our religious efforts trying to prove to him how great we are, and instead cast ourselves on his faithfulness. His faithfulness will produce more grace through us. He rewards us when we allow him to use us to distribute and broadcast his grace—and such rewards are simply another gift, a reward God gives as the icing on the cake, the crown he places on top of his own gift of grace.

This parable is an invitation to enter into the lavish grace of God as a way of life. It's an invitation to trust in him and thereby enter into his joy. This parable is also a warning for those who are, by virtue of trying to hoard God's grace, so busy digging their own spiritual graves that they fail to realize the grace they are desperately trying to keep for themselves is freely available to everyone.

CHAPTER 7

The Shrewd Operator

Jesus told his disciples: "There was a rich man whose manager was accused of wasting his possessions. So he called him in and asked him, 'What is this I hear about you? Give an account of your management, because you cannot be manager any longer.'

The manager said to himself, 'What shall I do now? My master is taking away my job. I'm not strong enough to dig, and I'm ashamed to beg— I know what I'll do so that, when I lose my job here, people will welcome me into their houses.'

So he called in each one of his master's debtors. He asked the first, 'How much do you owe my master?'

'Nine hundred gallons of olive oil,' he replied.

The manager told him, 'Take your bill, sit down quickly, and make it four hundred and fifty.'

Then he asked the second, 'And how much do you owe?'

'A thousand bushels of wheat,' he replied.

He told him, 'Take your bill and make it eight hundred.'

The master commended the dishonest manager because he had acted shrewdly. For the people of this world are more shrewd in dealing with their own kind than are the people of the light. I tell you, use worldly wealth to gain friends for yourselves, so that when it is gone, you will be welcomed into eternal dwellings.

Whoever can be trusted with very little can also be trusted with much, and whoever is dishonest with very little will also be dishonest with much. So if you have not been trustworthy in handling worldly wealth, who will trust you with true riches? And if you have not been trustworthy with someone else's property, who will give you property of your own?

No one can serve two masters. Either you will hate the one and love the other, or you will be devoted to the one and despise the other. You cannot serve both God and money.

The Pharisees, who loved money, heard all this and were sneering at Jesus. He said to them, "You are the ones who justify yourselves in the eyes of others, but God knows your hearts. What people value highly is detestable in God's sight."—Luke 16:1-15

I n the parable of the shrewd manager the hero is a supervisor/executive who is terminated from his job, yet he is praised by his boss (the rich man) for doing something even more crooked than what got him fired in the first place! The real spiritual lessons of this parable are nuanced, and for that reason the shrewd operator is seldom the topic of Sunday school lessons. There is far more to this parable than immediately meets the eye—in fact, in religious settings the deeper riches of God's grace that lie within this parable are often completely overlooked. Why does Jesus make a dishonest executive the hero of this parable? As we struggle with why Jesus praised a manager who wasted his employer's wealth, remember what Jesus had to say about a prodigal son who squandered the wealth he had just received from his father (we'll discuss more about Luke 15:11-32 in Chapter Eight).

Let's start by considering the details of this story much as we do those of a play. The two main characters are the rich man and his employee—his household manager whose job title also might be defined as a steward, overseer, supervisor, administrator or treasurer. The rich man discovers that his employee is wasting/losing money and fires him (or "sacks him" for British readers). The terminated manager devises a scheme whereby he might save his career.

Why does Jesus make a dishonest executive the hero of this parable?

He reduces the amount of debt owed by his former employer's debtors, before they can find out that he no longer has any authority to do so. The clever scheme seems to be successful, for 1) it obviously pleases those who owe money to his boss, 2) it makes his boss popular and well-liked and 3) makes friends for the now-terminated supervisor/ executive. Because it seems to be a win-win-win proposition, the boss commends the dishonest, former employee for being shrewd. Immediately following his parable Jesus concludes with six wisdom sayings—six morals to the story.

At the beginning of the parable the manager is charged with wasting the rich man's possessions, and later in the story Jesus calls him a *"dishonest manager."* We are not told exactly what the manager did. Was he cooking the books—keeping two sets of books, so that he could "skim" profits without the rich man knowing about it? If he was shrewd in coming up with a plan to save himself, we might assume that his original plan was also shrewd.

When the dishonest manager is caught with his hands in the cookie jar, Luke reveals the following about his thoughts:

• *"What shall I do now?"* he asks himself. He sees no way out other than to continue to rely on his own self-salvation scheme.

• He expresses no sorrow. He appears to be unable to face the truth about himself. Nothing leads us to think that he entertained the idea of coming clean, making an apology and offering to repay what he had wasted.

• At the very least, he knows he's guilty. He is "dead to rights."

• He admits he's lazy because he disdains manual labor. The blue-collar workers among the original audience who heard the character Jesus depicted as saying, *"I'm not strong enough to dig,"* must have relished hearing a white-collar guy admit that their lives really did consist of blood, sweat and tears. The terminated manager also admits that he's *"ashamed to beg."* However, as he considers another devious scam, it seems he's not ashamed to lie, cheat and steal.

The terminated manager hatches a plan to significantly reduce the amount others owe to his boss. Perhaps he had some clever version of the mortgage modification and reduction plans spawned by the housing bust during the first decade of the 21st century in North America. Perhaps this wheeling-and-dealing, terminated manager was a first-century predecessor of those we might call "insider traders" today. The first part of his scam/scheme to remove himself from deep do-do involves deceiving his former employer's debtors, so that they believe he still has authority over the rich man's possessions.

Who is Jesus praising as the hero? If God is the rich man, then who exactly is the immoral manager who cheats him?

The second step entails renegotiating with his former employer's debtors. In an attempt to remove his own "fingerprints" from these dubious transactions, the shrewd manager has the debtors write, in their own handwriting, the diminished sum they are only too willing to repay.

The shrewd manager seems to have at least one of two goals in mind: 1) become popular enough so that if his boss remains firm in his decision to terminate him, then this bold move of restructuring and downsizing debts will make him some new friends who might reward him by offering him a job, or 2) actually get back into the good graces of his boss. Perhaps he reasoned, if he made his rich-man boss popular, then even though such popularity came at a price, he would get his job back. At this point, the terminated manager must have felt he had nothing to lose.

The actions taken by the terminated manager effectively force the hand of his former boss. Once he found out about this latest scheme of his now terminated manager, the rich man could have decided to go to the debtors and explain that his former employee did not have the authority to reduce their debt, and they still owed him the difference between the illegally discounted, modified total and the original amount. However, taking back generosity everyone assumed he had given them would cost the rich man good will in the minds of those who owed him money.

On the other hand, the rich man could do nothing—and while the parable doesn't specifically say that he did so, we are left with the impression that he let the manager "get away" with his crime. Again, taken at strictly face value, this seems to be a mysterious parable.

Who is Jesus praising as the hero? If God is the rich man, then who exactly is the immoral manager who cheats him?

I believe that Jesus intended this mysterious parable to be yet another illustration of God's amazing grace. If a rich man forgives the crimes of one of his employees simply because it serves his own popularity to do so, then how much more can you count on the forgiveness of your heavenly Father who is willing to pay the full price for your salvation, even if it means he comes off looking like a weak fool?

Five Lessons

Immediately following the parable, Jesus gives five proverb-like morals-to-the-story by way of providing lessons to be learned from the parable:

Lesson # 1: *"For the people of this world are more shrewd in dealing with their own kind than are the people of the light"* (vs. 8).

If dishonest, shrewd crooks can "work the system" then why can't God's own children be smart enough to realize they can bank on God's grace? The parable points out that those who live in spiritual darkness are more likely to trust in human grace motivated by self-interest than those who live in the Light of Christ are in divine grace. This might be the core meaning of the parable, as this proverb-like statement is the first explanation Jesus offers.

Lesson # 2: *"I tell you, use worldly wealth to gain friends for yourselves, so that when it is gone, you will be welcomed into eternal dwellings"* (vs. 9).

I don't think the *"eternal dwellings"* to which Jesus has reference is the "place" we go to when we die. In the parable, when the terminated manager is concocting his plan, his goal is that *"people will welcome me into their houses"* (vs. 4). The terminated manager was smart enough to realize that employment opportunities don't last, but relationships do. He recognized a unique opportunity to capitalize on the riches of his former employer to build friendships. The terminated manager, facing a disaster, realized that the dividends earned by friendship easily outweigh and outlive dividends earned by wealth.

Lesson # 3: *"Whoever can be trusted with very little can also be trusted with much, and whoever is dishonest with very little will also be dishonest with much. So if you have not been trustworthy in handling worldly wealth, who will trust you with true riches? And if you have not been trustworthy with someone else's property, who will give you property of your own?"* (vs. 10-12).

There are actually three proverbs in these three sequential verses—each verse builds on itself, building a case for trust, brick by brick by brick. 1) In the kingdoms of this world, trust is normally given incrementally—and when someone proves himself/

herself trustworthy, then more trust is given. Logically, we assume if someone is untrustworthy in small things, if they ever are given more important responsibilities they will probably be untrustworthy with them as well (vs. 10). **2)** Again, logically, we might reason that those who are faithful with physical riches will be faithful with spiritual riches. (vs. 11). **3)** Finally, human wisdom leads us to conclude that if someone is untrustworthy with property that does not belong to them, why would someone give them their own property? (vs. 12).

But, given the context of God's grace, these questions seem designed to illustrate the enormous difference between the kingdoms of our world and the kingdom of heaven. God's grace is not earned—it is given, generously, as the rich man gave his grace in the parable. You can trust God to provide grace. Of course, the question is—can God trust those to whom he provides his grace? And the answer, borne of experience is—no, but then again, his thoughts and his ways are not like our own (Isaiah 55:8). That's why he is God and we are not. Were God to reserve his grace solely for those who have sufficient funds to pay the price, the doors of the kingdom of heaven would be forever sealed and secured, rather than open to one and all. Divine trust is not incrementally doled out as human trust is.

> **WERE God TO RESERVE HIS GRACE SOLELY FOR THOSE WHO HAVE SUFFICIENT FUNDS TO PAY THE PRICE, THE DOORS OF THE KINGDOM OF HEAVEN WOULD BE FOREVER SEALED AND SECURED, RATHER THAN OPEN TO ONE AND ALL.**

Lesson # 4: *"No one can serve two masters. Either you will hate the one and love the other, or you will be devoted to the one and despise the other. You cannot serve both God and money"* (vs. 13).

The currency of the kingdom of God is grace, whereas the currency of the kingdom of humanity is money, earned by hard work. The currency of the kingdom of religion is performance-based behavior. God spends his limitless grace in ways that appear foolhardy in the physical and spiritual kingdoms of humanity. God is not concerned about hoarding grace the way humans hoard their money. God is not impressed with a spiritual treasure chest filled with religious deeds. The true riches of God's grace are not acquired by means of money and commerce (physical or spiritual). God's grace liberates, whereas the currency of physical and religious economies enslave. As Jesus said in Matthew 6:21, *"For where your treasure is, there will your heart be also."*

> As far as the law-abiding, religious authorities were concerned, Jesus was playing fast and loose with their religious values.

Lesson # 5: *"The Pharisees, who loved money, heard all this and were sneering at Jesus. He said to them, 'You are the ones who justify yourselves in the eyes of others, but God knows your hearts. What people value highly is detestable in God's sight'"* (vs. 15).

While what humans value is detestable to God, the opposite is true as well. Jesus knew how the legalistic Pharisees would respond to this parable, and the proverbial lessons he offered by way of illustration.

The Pharisees despised the law-breaking, immoral manager of the parable who was able to weasel his way out of what he deserved because he appealed to what seemed to them a self-serving former boss. The Pharisees despised the manager because he broke the law and the rich man because he "caved in" and dispensed what many today label as soft-headed, easy-believism grace.

With this condemnation of the Pharisees, Jesus invites us to a deeper and more profound meaning of this parable. Who, humanly, did the Pharisees despise? According to the four Gospels, they were disgusted with Jesus, his message and all that he appeared to value. The religion of Jesus' day valued its own laws, customs, traditions and heritage. As far as the law-abiding, religious authorities were concerned, Jesus was playing fast and loose with their religious values. They respected hard work, and Jesus came to town preaching grace. They hated Jesus because his gospel of grace would liberate those who were enslaved to their religious laws and methodologies.

The Pharisees despised Jesus, because he broke their laws (which they, of course, believed were one and the same as God's laws). He hung out with homeless, lazy and law-breaking failures. Jesus seemed to genuinely like losers, while the religious leaders saw losers as being cursed by God for their bad behavior.

The Pharisees felt that Jesus didn't get losers into line with respectable religion. In the eyes of the religion of his day, Jesus lowered standards by consorting with hated tax collectors, prostitutes, dirty and untrustworthy shepherds, women and children. Beyond that, Jesus expressed and demonstrated compassion to the sick and diseased, most of whom the Pharisees believed to be flawed failures, paying a deserved penalty for their sins.

It seemed to the religious leaders that Jesus devalued the very things they valued—and they were right! After all, *"what people value highly is detestable in God's sight"* (vs. 15). It wasn't long after Jesus finished teaching this parable that these proud, arrogant, self-righteous religious leaders did to Jesus exactly what they felt should have been done to the manager in the parable.

God's grace is the most terrifying thing in the world to those who live in spiritual darkness.

CHAPTER 8

A Field Trip to a "Holy" Place

As he taught, Jesus said, "Watch out for the teachers of the law. They like to walk around in flowing robes and be greeted with respect in the marketplaces, and have the most important seats in the synagogues and the places of honor at banquets. They devour widows' houses and for a show make lengthy prayers. These men will be punished most severely."

Jesus sat down opposite the place where the offerings were put and watched the crowd putting their money into the temple treasury. Many rich people threw in large amounts. But a poor widow came and put in two very small copper coins, worth only a few cents.

Calling his disciples to him, Jesus said, "Truly I tell you, this poor widow has put more into the treasury than all the others. They all gave out of their wealth; but she, out of her poverty, put in everything—all she had to live on." —Mark 12:38-44

Misunderstanding the Bible is so easy. In fact, misunderstanding the Bible is more than easy, it is inevitable! To the degree that we uncritically allow religious authorities to tell us exactly what the Bible means and what it doesn't, then detours from an objective and balanced understanding of the Bible are inescapable.

What exactly is the point of Jesus' teaching about the widow who, in his words, *"out of her poverty, put in everything"* into the temple treasury—and again, why did he say that she contributed *"all she had to live on"*?

Is Jesus commending the widow's example, telling us that we should go and do likewise? Is he saying that we should give until it hurts, giving all we have to live on? Variations of that idea are, by far and away, the most common explanation of this passage of Scripture.

Along with so many other pastors and teachers within Christendom, I have, in the past, quoted this passage as if Jesus' intent in this passage is for us to give until it hurts—giving, as the widow did, *"all she had to live on."*

About a year or so ago, a pastor friend of mine emailed me and asked me about something I had said about this passage we often call, using the language employed by the 1611 King James Version, *"the widow's mite."* In more modern versions, like the New International Version, her offering is said to have consisted of *"two very small copper coins, worth only a few cents."*

My friend had been reading something I wrote, and while I hadn't fully explained this passage, I briefly mentioned it as if it were an example of Jesus praising the widow for giving *"all she had to live on."* My friend challenged me to study this passage in a little more detail. After doing so, I discovered my previous perspective of this passage was wrong.

Setting the Record Straight

By God's grace, allow me to set the record straight and help you in any misunderstanding you have had of this passage of Scripture—whether you received that misleading perspective from me or from others. What is the real lesson Jesus wants us to understand about the widow's offering? One of the most basic and foundational rules of understanding anyone (whether they are speaking or writing) is to allow their words to be explained by the context.

Today the media likes what it calls "sound bites" (short, brief statements that someone said or wrote) for several reasons. One reason the media favors sound bites is that readers and listeners are lazy. Readers and listeners don't want to take the time, even if it's two or three minutes, to discover the context of what someone said or wrote. We 21st-century North Americans want a quick, abbreviated summary—short and sweet.

Another reason the media favors sound bites is that our attention span—the time we are able to concentrate and focus on a message—has been greatly diminished by so many voices that clamor for our attention. We are used to getting a quick, brief and to-the-point answer or explanation. It's a fast food mentality isn't it? When it comes to fast food, we want to drive up to the speaker, place our order and then within a minute or two, drive up to the window, pay our money and receive what we requested.

We don't want a lecture about nutrition, we just want to quickly eat and drink something that will make us feel full. When it comes to information, knowledge and wisdom, our society is geared the same way. Make it quick and easy.

Given this desire, those who cater to our consumer-driven culture—whether they are selling news in a magazine, newspaper, on the radio or television—whether they are teaching in a high school or college—whether they are teaching and explaining the Bible—are tempted to make it "quick and easy." Thus some go to church and say, "just give me the spiritual equivalent of a hamburger or burrito. Make it quick and easy. No thinking please. No big words—no long explanations."

Because spiritual consumers are not discriminating, there is a whole lot of mis-information and dis-information out there. Within Christendom there are many churches that encourage those who attend to check their brains at the door of the church. They don't encourage questions—in fact some even discourage and criticize those who ask questions. "Quick and easy" is one of the enemies of truth.

That said, back to our passage about the widow's offering. Let's take just a few moments to carefully consider what was taking place that provides the background for this passage. We're going to see that Jesus was giving a caution to both his disciples and to all readers of the Bible down through time. Immediately following the warning, Jesus took them on a field trip to illustrate the lesson he had just given.

At the beginning of this chapter, I quoted the longer passage (Mark 12:38-44) that provides the

116

immediate context for the field trip on which Jesus took his disciples. Most teachers and preachers neglect to include the background, favoring just the example of the widow's offering (vs. 41-44) and then scold those who do not give "enough." Such interpretations assume that the widow's offering is the lesson Jesus was giving. But the widow's offering was the field trip—it was a real life, religious illustration of the lesson that was already given!

The Lesson

The lesson of this longer passage is given in verses 38-40. Jesus explained that the big religious dogs like to draw attention to themselves by their clothing. The religious hot shots liked to be given places of honor at banquets and in religious places of worship, which were, or course, synagogues in that culture. These religious authorities craved and lived for the respectful greeting they would hear from others, including all their titles and degrees. These religious professionals loved the admiration of others. They gave long and pompous prayers as they attempted to impress.

And then Jesus said, in addition to all of that, they *"devour widows' houses."* How did those religious leaders *"devour widows' houses"*? In that day, widows were almost always impoverished. Today men and women have desired skills and qualifications, and the ability to be employed—if work is available. But in those days the husband was the sole provider. Without a husband a widow had to rely on the generosity and charity of others.

Widows are vulnerable in a variety of ways. They grieve the loss of their husbands, and in that emotional state humans are not capable of making

117

the best decisions. People who have just endured a great loss are easily manipulated. What did Jesus mean when he condemned V.I.P. religious leaders who preyed on the little people, in his words, *"devouring widows' houses?"*

I believe Jesus was condemning anyone who used the guise of religion to solicit monies from people who could ill afford to give. I believe Jesus was decrying the exploitation of the weak and the impoverished.

Jesus is condemning the unethical and unconscionable abuse of the little people—the impoverished.

Jesus was denouncing institutions that bankrupt and further impoverish those whom they ostensibly serve. Jesus was warning that the big business of religion can devour vulnerable people by appealing to their desire to give to God, metaphorically raping and pillaging just as a victorious army might do to the people they have just conquered in battle.

It's not a pretty picture, is it? Here Jesus, in no uncertain words, is saying that those who were esteemed by many people as being virtuous were fleecing the very flock they were presumably serving.

The classroom lecture Jesus gave to his disciples is one which all Christ-centered teachers must take to heart. Those of us who teach must never unscrupulously work on the emotions of vulnerable and hurting people. When a church or a ministry needs financial support, it may ask—after all— Jesus said *"ask and it will be given to you"* (Matthew 7:7). There is nothing wrong with making monetary needs known. How it is done is another matter.

Jesus is condemning the unethical and un-conscionable abuse of the little people— the impoverished. Devouring someone else's house in the name of God is the every opposite of everything Jesus taught. After giving that clear message, Jesus then took his disciples on a field trip to the majestic temple to see a poor widow's offering.

Read verses 41-44 carefully. Jesus doesn't supply details about what motivated this woman to give *"everything—all she had to live on."* She could have been giving everything she had out of her love for God. Or she could have been acting out of guilt and fear. She could also have been vain about what she was doing. Jesus doesn't comment on her attitude or motivation.

The Field Trip

After Jesus gave a lecture to his disciples (as well as a *"large crowd"*—vs. 37), condemning religious leaders for devouring widows' houses (vs. 40), it seems logical that he would then take them on a field trip to illustrate such abuse. But why the temple? The temple was the center of all religion at that time, and it was in the temple that Jesus provided an illustration of how widows' houses were being devoured, in the name of God.

The commonly accepted explanation that Jesus was pointing to the generosity of this impoverished widow as a way of shaming Christians into giving everything to God (or to those who claim to be his earthly representatives) is flawed, and beyond that, manipulative.

Jesus was condemning morally bankrupt religious leaders and their institutions who bamboozle their followers into thinking financial sacrifices will result in their ticket being punched for heaven. The poor widow was an illustration of religion constructing its magnificent edifices on the backs of the poor.

Turn on your television—you can see this kind of spiritually corrupt message broadcast virtually every day. It's called "seed faith" by some—the idea is that the money you give to the preacher and the ministry will be multiplied, so that you receive back from God far more than you give to the radio/television ministry!

Jesus is using the widow as a case in point, warning those who prey on the fears and anxieties of those who are grieving and suffering, and who yearn to believe that God will reward their financial sacrifices by welcoming them into the kingdom of heaven.

Jesus is unequivocally condemning religious leaders when they *"devour widows' houses."* Jesus is not happy with the *"depraved conduct"* of greedy religious teachers who exploit others and *"bring the way of truth into disrepute"* (2 Peter 2:2-3).

Time and time again Jesus revealed his love and ministry for those who were vulnerable, those who were bruised reeds (Matthew 12:20). His ministry was dedicated to those who were and are physically and spiritually oppressed, imprisoned, impoverished and blind (Luke 4:18). He, God in the flesh, willingly experienced the hardships and deprivations of those he served. When we, his followers, physically and spiritually clothe the naked, visit prisoners and the sick and feed the hungry and thirsty, we are doing it to and for him (Matthew 25:40).

Just as a ministry today that provides food and medication for sick and hungry children might provide a photograph of the misery and suffering such children endure, Jesus took his disciples to the opulent and lavish temple, and pointed out a defenseless, preyed upon woman who was in religious bondage. This widow was being destroyed by an unrelenting religious system that demanded more and more and more.

> **Jesus is delivering a powerful, no-nonsense warning to spiritual scam-artists and widow-devourers.**

This field trip provided a real life example of a vulnerable widow whose "house" was devoured by religion.

Jesus took his disciples to watch an impoverished widow give. Given that his lecture just before this "field trip" was all about religious exploitation we have to consider the possibility that this widow had been browbeaten and shamed into giving, as Jesus said, *"all she had to live on"* (vs. 44).

Jesus is delivering a powerful, no-nonsense warning to spiritual scam-artists and widow-devourers. Jesus gives the widow as an example of a religious victim—and in so doing he is providing clear, unambiguous teaching that no human being should ever feel obligated to give everything they have to a church or ministry. Jesus is warning us that Christless religion can be cruel and ruthless, causing deep physical and spiritual suffering. Jesus is cautioning about the smokescreens, illusions and false promises of empty religion, which will always attempt to enslave its followers to legalistic rituals and ceremonies.

Before we leave this powerful lesson, we should consider whether the disciples got the point. They heard the powerful lecture Jesus gave and then accompanied Jesus on the field trip to the temple to see the impoverished victim of institutionalized religion.

Did they appreciate the deep and profound teaching Jesus gave them? Here's the next verse:

As he was leaving the temple, one of his disciples said to him, *"Look, Teacher! What massive stones! What magnificent buildings!"*(Mark 13:1).

Years ago, after delivering what I believed to be a spellbinding lecture, filled with colorful illustrations and obvious lessons, a student raised his hand, yawned and asked me, "Uh—will this be on the test?" Reality bites! Jesus has just gone to great lengths to point out this victim who had been devoured and abused, who had put all that she had to live on into the temple treasury. One of his disciples looked around—as if what Jesus had said went in one proverbial ear and out the other—and said, "Wow, check out this religious edifice. This temple is incredibly beautiful."

In his sermon at Nazareth Jesus Christ announced, as recorded in the fourth chapter of the Gospel of Luke (Luke 4:18), that his mission was all about preaching good news to the poor—that would include impoverished widows. He came to proclaim freedom for the prisoners. Without diminishing the terrible circumstances of physical prisoners, there are far more spiritual prisoners who are held in spiritual places of bondage.

Jesus came to proclaim freedom and to release the oppressed. He mentioned nothing whatsoever in his sermon in Nazareth about coming to this earth so that his followers could build expensive, huge and ornate cathedrals or mega-churches. Jesus didn't come to build cathedrals or "save the temple." In fact, Jesus prophesied that the temple in Jerusalem where the widow put in all that she had, the temple whose beauty and grandeur caused the disciples to be amazed, would be utterly destroyed—*"not one stone here will be left on another; every one will be thrown down"* (Mark 13:2).

It's sad that the disciples were not appalled at the fact that the impoverished widow might have given everything she had because she had been manipulated by greedy religious professionals who devoured widows' houses. It's sad that the disciples could only be impressed by a religious building, rather than the deep and profound, life-giving freedom of the gospel of Jesus, which releases people from the tyranny of religion.

It's gratifying to read that these same disciples, spiritually transformed and Spirit-filled after the resurrection of Jesus, were far more motivated to provide *for* widows rather than appropriate *from* them.

The Member and the Non-Member

To some who were confident of their own right-eousness and looked down on everyone else, Jesus told this parable: "Two men went up to the temple to pray, one a Pharisee and the other a tax collec-tor. The Pharisee stood by himself and prayed: 'God, I thank you that I am not like other people—robbers, evildoers, adulterers—or even like this tax collec-tor. I fast twice a week and give a tenth of all I get.'

"But the tax collector stood at a distance. He would not even look up to heaven, but beat his breast and said, 'God, have mercy on me, a sinner.'

"I tell you that this man, rather than the oth-er, went home justified before God. For all those who exalt themselves will be humbled, and those who humble themselves will be exalted." —Luke 18:9-14

Good guys are usually upstanding, law-keeping moral people and bad guys are cheating, conniving, money grubbers. The original audience who first heard Jesus weave this masterful parable of the Pharisee and the tax collector would have immediately thought of the Pharisee as the good guy. Pharisees were, among other things, the first-century equivalent of 21st-century involved church members who are always in attendance at church, always participating and generously giving of their time, talents and treasures.

It was a no-brainer for the first-century audience to identify the bad guy in this parable. Everyone knew about dishonest, swindling, corrupt tax collectors—their profession was known for ripping people off. So the audience who first heard this parable would have immediately cast the tax collector in the role of the bad guy.

When it came to religion—those who first heard this parable knew that the tax collector, by reason of his profession, was obviously a non-member—someone who rarely, if ever, went to church. One of the comparisons Jesus draws of these two men is that the church member, assumed to be the good guy, seems to have felt right at home in church and that God was in his hip pocket. On the other hand, the non-member, the presumed bad guy, didn't even feel he deserved for God to notice him.

Benefitting from almost 2,000 years of hindsight, we realize that Jesus was turning the tables on that original audience, teaching them a lesson by deliberately choosing the most unlikely characters to play the good guy and the bad guy. So today we reverse the roles, and see the prayer of the Pharisee as pretentious and filled with pride. We think of the Pharisee as the bad buy—a self-righteous, proud and arrogant legalist. And we smugly congratulate ourselves: "Thank God we're not like him!"

But wait, he was self-righteous, proud and arrogant but also faithfully tithed and attended church. He was the very kind of person that most churches today are looking for as a member, was he not? And as for the low-down no-good tax collector (the one Jesus made the hero of this parable) well, let's get real. He would not be someone most churches would go out of their way to recruit as a member, would he?

We know that this greedy money hungry rip-off artist is the good guy of the parable, but most churches would not want anyone remotely like him as a member. His presence in their church might make everyone else look bad. A cheater, a swindler —someone like Bernie Madoff—no, most churches would not try to convince such a person to join their church. In the in-speak of many churches today, the hero of this parable is a non-member.

Who Are All These Non-Members?

Let's assume this corrupt public official who extorted money from his own people visited a church today—at very best most churches and pastors would see him as a conversion project. He definitely would not be viewed as one of "us"—he would be a "them." Have you ever thought of the words institutional Christianity uses to describe non-members—people who are on the "them" side of the "them" and "us" divide?

Here's a few terms used to describe spiritually unsavory types who are non-members: *un-saved, un-believer, un-converted, un-regenerate*. Some churchgoers might describe non-members as those who are *in the world—those who don't know the truth.* Depending on the church a person goes to, non-members might even be called *pagans*. Of course, to be fair, giving a pagan the benefit of the doubt, a pagan might be someone who doesn't know "the truth" and thus doesn't know any better. In some churches non-members who attend infrequently, in contrast to the members who attend virtually every week, are belittled with the label *pew-warmers*. Others prefer to speak of those they presume to be spiritual slackers as *back-sliders.*

The underlying attitude that infects much of Christendom is that if pathetic non-member slobs knew better, they would be more like us, and probably a member of our church. This attitude motivates much of what is known as "evangelism"—recruiting efforts to get the poor, sin-sick, unredeemed into church. When some churches instruct their members to "evangelize" outsiders, when they try to convert a non-member into a member, their motivation is not just to get them to accept Jesus Christ, but their motivation is to increase the membership of their church.

For after all, a foundational premise of evangelism, even if it is unstated, is that our religious club is better than other religious clubs. In fact, some churches even regard other churches and their members as *un-saved, un-believers and un-converted.*

In Jesus' parable the Pharisee prayed, *"God, I thank you that I am not like other people—robbers, evildoers, adulterers—or even like this tax collector."*

In religious settings today the prayer often becomes, "God, I thank you that I am not like those Episcopalians, who don't even read—and certainly don't obey—the Bible."

Or, "God, I thank you I am not like those illiterate emotional Pentecostals."

Or, "God I thank you I am a Christian, and not like those Muslims or Buddhists."

Or even, "God, I thank you I am not like one of those self-righteous, arrogant legalists—I thank you that I understand your grace."

That's one of the most destructive prayers of all— "thank you I am not like the Pharisee in the parable who thanked you that he was not like others. Thank you I am not a Pharisee!" How spiritually blind can we get?

Them Versus Us

Playing the "them" versus "us" game is seductive and dangerous—it leads us away from the humility, love and grace of Christ into prideful religion. But we all play the game, because part of being human means that we are predisposed to look down on others who are not like us. Apart from Christ, we're all like that.

"Them" against "us" is a spiritual virus—it leads to wars between nations, as nations look down on each other and condemn each other. For example, we North Americans rightly remember the horrible tragedy of 9-11—when over 3,000 civilian lives were taken by cowardly terrorists, whose hatred was fueled by religion. But we often don't think much about the tens of thousands who have died in the warfare that resulted from 9-11.

Why don't we? Well, deep down, many North American Christians believe that their nation is better than predominantly Muslim countries. Intrinsic to all humans, and to all religion, is the conviction we all believe that our lives are worth more than others. The virus of exalting ourselves above others—playing the spiritually lethal game of "them" against "us"—ultimately leads to hatred and violence. Wars, in the name of God, are fought because of conclusions based on the deadly virus of "them" versus "us."

It is apparent that many Muslims believe themselves, if not their religion, to be morally superior to the religion favored by most North Americans. Restrained, at least to some degree, by our sense of democracy, political correctness and fair play, many North Americans do not answer in kind—but silently believe Islam is a religion of terrorists.

> Playing the "them" versus "us" game is seductive and dangerous— it leads us away from the humility, love and grace of Christ into prideful religion.

Thus it seems that many Muslims pray, "God, I thank you I am not like the corrupt infidels of the West."

And, it also seems that many within Christendom pray, "God, I thank you that I am not like those closed-minded, hateful Muslims."

There are many who read this parable and thank God that they are not like those hard-hearted, conservative, legalistic, proud, self-righteous Christians who go to church a few blocks away. Of course, when and if we say or think something to that effect, it may well be that our own words condemn us (Matthew 12:37). It may well be that what we are thanking God we *are not* is the very thing we *are*! Jesus teaches us in this parable that it is futile to grade others on the basis of who we think they are, who they seem to be, and how we believe they fall short of acceptable religious standards. Anytime we fall for the seductive pleasure of comparing ourselves favorably with another human being, we become spiritual scorekeepers.

The Pharisee in the parable maintained accurate records of the shortcomings of others. When he compared himself to others, he invariably came out of his little game of "them" and "us" smelling like a spiritual rose. The little phrase in the parable, when the Pharisee is described as praying *about himself* is a huge clue about this pitfall which we have all experienced—and apart from the humility of Christ, as he lives his life in us, it's a religious pit into which we will continually fall.

This whole attitude of scorekeeping is the foundation of gossip. We love to gossip about the sordid lives of others, while remaining oblivious of our own shortcomings. We love to read and listen to sleaze about celebrities—or, even better, someone we know or someone who goes to our church—or, perhaps best of all, someone who *used to* go to our church, and now, because they no longer do all the religious stuff we do, we sigh about what a mess they are in. After all, their lives have to be a big mess because they are no longer like us!

The church world has many terms for people who used to be a member of a particular church, but left, or who were asked to leave. Today, the term *unchurched* is a popular way to speak of non-members or former members.

On the surface, the term *unchurched* seems to be somewhat neutral and tolerant. But the truth is, using the term *unchurched* often communicates deep, unseen layers of judgment and condemnation toward those who don't frequent a building which calls itself a church.

Historically, churches have referred to former members who became *unchurched* as *apostates*—literally meaning, "one who has abandoned religious faith." *Heretics* is another popular term used about non-members—meaning someone who has accepted beliefs and practices that are contrary to the accepted views of the religion accepted by the majority.

When action is necessary to remove a bad apple heretic from the flock, *excommunication* has been favored by Catholics.

The Amish, and others, use the term *shunning*. *Shunning* is the command given to current members by their hierarchy about avoiding former members. *Shunning* includes the actions of avoiding, despising, renouncing and even scorning someone who used to be part of your group.

Some groups use the word *disfellowship*. To be "in fellowship" includes being a dues-paying, compliant follower of the group. When and if someone stops paying their dues and conforming to all the rules and regulations, they are *disfellowshipped*.

Disconnect is a term I only heard recently in this context. As I understand its use and definition, *disconnect* is the decree, given by a particular authoritarian religious group, commanding its followers to withdraw, separate and disassociate themselves from someone they once regarded as their spiritual friend and associate. The order comes down from on high—*disconnect* and disassociate yourself from these heretics and apostates.

While there is a time and place for church discipline, so the weak and vulnerable in a fellowship may be protected, protecting the innocent can become a license for tyranny. Religious pride and superiority are as far from the teachings of Jesus as east is from west. The big business of religion loves to pray about itself—or even to itself—thanking God that it is not like others. I believe this "them" versus "us" virus is part of the reason why testimonies are so popular in some churches.

Some churches include public testimonies in their services—really juicy personal stories told by someone who used to be really bad, but now that person has repented. It's called their *testimony*— and when it comes time for salacious testimonies some sit there in the church and think "God, I thank you I've never been *that* bad."

I don't mean to say that some church-goers are not genuinely delighted when God dramatically and miraculously, by his grace, transforms someone's life. Of course, I believe that the reaction of real Christians, in whom Christ lives, is closer to "there but for the grace of God go I."

The "them versus us" game is an inherited spiritual virus—an innate desire we have to elevate our own spiritual standing by favorably comparing ourselves with someone who seems to us to be a loser and a failure. This spiritual virus causes us to compare ourselves (and thus to feel good about ourselves) with someone whom we feel is a much greater sinner than we are. Sure, we admit we're sinners, but not *that* bad!

The core teaching of this parable is no matter who we are, no matter what we have done, no matter what we are now doing—all of us, apart from him, are spiritually dead. We have no spiritual life apart from Jesus.

The other core teaching at the heart of this parable is that God loves everyone, because of his goodness, not based on the performance of those who presume to earn his favor.

But Does God Really Love Everyone?

People who are held in bondage to religion will almost universally agree—"of course, God loves everyone—he just loves those who are in my religion more. Of course, God loves us all equally— it's just that the members of my church are more equal than others."

Within Christendom, the prayer "God, I thank you I am not like others" often turns into a comparison of those who seem to be Christians and those who seem not to be. It's another variation of the "them" versus "us" spiritual virus.

The discussion often goes something like this: "Sure, God loves the entire world. Sure, Jesus died for the entire world. But only those who accept Jesus Christ are saved. So, God must love those of us who are Christians more than others."

But here's the problem. When we start making determinations of who is a Christian and who is not a Christian, we are entering into a sphere where angels fear to tread. But Christ-less religion doesn't fear to tread there, does it?

God has not invited us to make determinations based on our observations, our knowledge or our perceptions as to what he is doing and how he reveals himself to others.

Though Christ-less religion seems to be preoccupied with making dogmatic statements about what God is doing (how he reveals himself to others—and how and when he makes his love known to others) such determinations are none of our business!

One of the most misunderstood and most abused scriptures in all the Bible is perhaps the most memorized and most quoted—John 3:16:

"For God so loved the world that he gave his one and only Son, that whoever believes in him shall not perish but have eternal life."

CHRISTIANS CAN'T ACCURATELY IDENTIFY THOSE WHO HAVE ACCEPTED GOD'S GRACE AND THOSE WHO HAVEN'T.

It seems, on the surface, that this verse clearly states that God gave his one and only Son so that people would not perish. So, many good, church-going folks reason, if people don't respond to God's love, then they will perish. And then, often encouraged by hell-fire-and-brimstone sermons about a hell of eternal torture, folks start to think about all those people who are perishing.

The number of people that religious folks think are perishing has a direct relationship to the numbers of people who are not a part of their church or their denomination. Seemingly good, church-going folks (sort of like the Pharisee) conclude that those who are perishing are "them"—they are not "us." Many of them don't look like "our" members. They don't dress like "our" members. They don't practice the same rituals and ceremonies "our" members do.

So, in many cases:

• instead of reading John 3:16 and thanking God for his all inclusive love,

• instead of thanking him that he will, in his own time and his own way, express his love and make his love known to the whole world,

Many read John 3:16 and pray the Pharisee's prayer: "God, I thank you I am not like all those miserable people who are perishing because they are not members of my church."

One of the great lessons we can learn from the parable of the Pharisee and the tax collector is that neither individual Christians nor organized groups of Christians have been given the keys to unlock the love of God for those who do not seem to be enjoying and experiencing it. Christians can't accurately identify those who have accepted God's grace and those who haven't. We do not exclusively possess God's love and grace—we can experience it and enjoy it, but we don't own it. By grace, in Christ, we can participate in a relationship with God, but we do not monopolize his love. We do not decide to whom God will express his love nor how and when he will do so.

We are all in need of God's grace. May we all truly be thankful for his love and his grace, as he has revealed it to us. May we give thanks that we may rest in him, assured that he will, and for that matter, in many cases, already has, made that same love available to many others—even though we are unaware of it. May we rest in his grace!

CHAPTER 10

A Father's Unreserved & Undeserved Love

Jesus continued: "There was a man who had two sons. The younger one said to his father, 'Father, give me my share of the estate.' So he divided his property between them.

Not long after that, the younger son got together all he had, set off for a distant country and there squandered his wealth in wild living. After he had spent everything, there was a severe famine in that whole country, and he began to be in need. So he went and hired himself out to a citizen of that country, who sent him to his fields to feed pigs. He longed to fill his stomach with the pods that the pigs were eating, but no one gave him anything.

When he came to his senses, he said, 'How many of my father's hired servants have food to spare, and here I am starving to death! I will set out and go back to my father and say to him: Father, I have sinned against heaven and against you. I am no longer wor-

thy to be called your son; make me like one of your hired servants.' So he got up and went to his father.

But while he was still a long way off, his father saw him and was filled with compassion for him; he ran to his son, threw his arms around him and kissed him.

The son said to him, 'Father, I have sinned against heaven and against you. I am no longer worthy to be called your son.'

But the father said to his servants, 'Quick! Bring the best robe and put it on him. Put a ring on his finger and sandals on his feet. Bring the fattened calf and kill it. Let's have a feast and celebrate. For this son of mine was dead and is alive again; he was lost and is found.' So they began to celebrate.

Meanwhile, the older son was in the field. When he came near the house, he heard music and dancing. So he called one of the servants and asked him what was going on. 'Your brother has come,' he replied, 'and your father has killed the fattened calf because he has him back safe and sound.'

The older brother became angry and refused to go in. So his father went out and pleaded with him. But he answered his father, 'Look! All these years I've been slaving for you and never disobeyed your orders. Yet you never gave me even a young goat so I could celebrate with my friends. But when this son of yours who has squandered your property with prostitutes comes home, you kill the fattened calf for him!'

'My son,' the father said, 'you are always with me, and everything I have is yours. But we had to celebrate and be glad, because this brother of yours was dead and is alive again; he was lost and is found.'" —Luke 15: 11-32 keep coming back to the parable of the prodigal/lost son. As I continue to reflect on this parable, I am always learning something new. For many years I saw this story as primarily about our heavenly Father forgiving us, as his sons and daughters.

I now believe that forgiveness is only a part of the message. Forgiveness is a consequence of God's love. Far more than simply being a parable about forgiveness, it's a story about a father's unreserved and undeserved love.

The forgiveness illustrated in this parable flows out of the father's love. The younger, prodigal son is not forgiven because he does something "religious"—crawling on his hands and knees, paying penance, lighting candles, putting ashes on his forehead, following a program, praying without ceasing, fasting at least once a week, etc. The son is forgiven because the father loves him, not because he does something to activate or rejuvenate or earn his father's love.

• The father's love is *unreserved*—it knows no boundaries.

• The father's love is *undeserved*—it cannot be gained or attained on the basis of human performance.

The younger son is forgiven because the father is helplessly and hopelessly in love with his son. The story related in the parable is all about a celebration of love.

The father welcomes his youngest son home —he gives him the best robe, he places a ring on his finger and he gives instructions for the fattened calf to be killed so that they can feast—all in celebration of love!

It's truly a story of God's unrestrained and unbridled love. The word "prodigal" is an old English word having to do with lavish, excessive, extravagant and sumptuous. Prodigal also includes the idea of "wasteful" and indeed, that's the way the "prodigal" son is introduced in the parable. He wasted his father's generosity (the son had no right to ask for his share of the estate ahead of time).

> God's love is lavish, EXCESSIVE, EXTRAVAGANT AND SUMPTUOUS— AND IN THAT REGARD God is A PRODIGAL God.

But the father's love is more than a match for his son's wastefulness—it is impossible for the son to squander and dissipate his father's love! God's love is lavish, excessive, extravagant and sumptuous— and in that regard God is a prodigal God.

We need to remember the context of this parable. Jesus was teaching the undesirables—the untouchables, the unloved, moral outcasts and discredited people like tax collectors (Luke 15:2) —when the religious teachers expressed their disapproval of what he was doing.

Jesus responds, via three parables, to the religious condemnation of his ministry, and the fact that he spent time with the least, the lost and the last. Some Bibles title these three parables as the lost sheep, the lost coin and the lost son.

Perhaps these three parables should be seen as three acts of one drama about God's amazing grace and endless love, about being spiritually lost and found.

The Most Famous and Perfect Parable?

The parable of the loving father and his two sons is not only one of the most famous stories Jesus ever told, it may be the most perfect—for it is a telling story of our lives. We often read this drama and think that it's about only one of the sons—and we often think that he was the only one who was lost. As it turns out, both of the sons were lost, in different ways.

Circumstances forced the younger son to face the inescapable conclusion he was lost and needed to be rescued. Meanwhile, by way of contrast, his older brother who thought he was safe at home was actually just as lost, spiritually. The two brothers, apart from God's love and grace, are a perfect illustration of the futility of humanity living apart from God, living without relationship with God.

Jesus starts his parable with the younger, more reckless son. The younger son requests his share of the family assets so that he can leave home and make his way in the world. In asking for "his share," the younger son was effectively saying that he could not stand to live at home with his father, and that he wanted "his share" of the estate before it was rightfully his—before his father died.

Normally, the father would have the use of those funds to take care of himself and the rest of his family in his old age. What the young son was asking for constitutes a radical rejection of the father and all that his father stood for.

The father did not refuse his younger son's request, even though it was disrespectful, ungrateful, self-centered, greedy and immature.

The young man wanted money, not property. He wanted, as humans naturally do, instant gratification. The younger son didn't ask for the family farm. He wasn't interested in milking cows, cleaning the barn and painting fences for the rest of his life. He wasn't thinking about honor or tradition or respect of the family name—he just wanted the money—now!

The original audience would have been amazed at the father's response. In order to give his son an inheritance ahead of time, the father would have needed to sell part of his land.

In 21st-century North America people don't give a second thought to selling a home or a piece of real estate. Land is simply another asset to be used, leveraged for loans and eventually sold. But land, in the first-century culture, particularly given the old covenant promises about the land God promised, was closely tied to a person's identity.

THE FACT THAT THE FATHER WAS WILLING TO GIVE HIS SON EXACTLY WHAT HE ASKED FOR WAS AN AMAZING PART OF THIS STORY TO THE FIRST-CENTURY AUDIENCE.

When the father put up a "for sale" sign on 1/3 of the acreage, the neighbors would have been aghast. On the part of the younger son, simply asking that his father be willing to publicly humiliate himself in such a way signals his desire to end the identity he had with his father and his family. While no details are given, the fact that the father was willing to give his son exactly what he asked for was an amazing part of this story to the first-century audience.

As we move through this story, the father's love is the one constant. This parable is about God's unconditional and boundless love—his amazing grace. In the case of the younger son, it's about those who are lost because they have chosen to be lost, yet the Father still loves them.

The father's *unreserved and undeserved* love makes this parable a problem for religion that conditions its favors and rewards upon strict obedience. Christless religion operates on the principle, as all religion does, of *quid pro quo*. Religion believes that as and when we humans scratch God's back, he will respond and scratch ours. God's unlimited and unconditional love causes huge cracks to form in the foundation of religion—its effect is like a 9.0 earthquake striking the hallowed halls of legalistic religion.

The younger son left for a distant country and squandered the wealth his father had given him in wild living. But, as it turns out, he could run but he could not hide from his father's love. God still loves us even when we run away from him. No specifics are given, but in general we can assume that as long as the younger son had money he had many friends. But, when the money ran out so did the fair-weather friends.

Later on, when the younger son returned home, his older brother accused him of squandering their father's property with prostitutes. Given the details of the story, this specific allegation is unfounded— the parable does not stipulate one way or another that this was the kind of life in which the younger son indulged. When religion collides with God's grace, the only thing it can do is to disparage, devalue and discredit. Religious legalism cannot fathom or understand the unconditional love of God.

The younger brother ran out of money and in desperation became a hired hand on a pig farm. Working with pigs was about as low as any young Jewish man could go—pigs, and those who raised them, were an abomination. But it was the only work he could find.

We can imagine how scandalized the first-century religious leaders were when they heard how low this son had sunk. Yet, the real scandal (to the human mind) was when Jesus said that the father never stopped loving his son no matter what his son had done or was doing. That was the real scandal for religion—and it still is! God keeps loving us no matter what. God's love is an endless, no-matter-what love, in complete contrast with the values, beliefs and teachings of legalistic religion.

> THE REAL SCANDAL (TO THE HUMAN MIND) WAS WHEN JESUS SAID THE FATHER NEVER STOPPED LOVING HIS SON NO MATTER WHAT HIS SON HAD DONE OR WAS DOING.

The Bible says that it was in this low spiritual place that the younger son came to himself. The young man decided to go home—his idea was that he would ask his father for a job—reasoning that if he was going to work like or as a slave, he might as well do so for his father.

He knew that his father treated the hired hands with respect and love and any gesture of kindness or acceptance would be welcome news for this disgraced and impoverished son. The son did not dream of asking his father to restore him to a position of grace.

The son did not, in a million years, expect his father to react to him as graciously as he did. The younger son merely wanted to say that he was sorry. Given what he had done, he could only hope that his father would forgive him.

He was willing to swallow his pride and come home. Having left with his pockets full of money, snubbing his nose at the relationship that his father offered him—now this repentant and remorseful son returned in rags, in abject poverty, willing to be mocked and scorned by his community. He fully expected that he would need to reimburse his father with installment payments for the inheritance he had squandered.

Out of his love, the father respected his son's choice... He did not hire bounty hunters to kidnap his son and bring him home.

It's interesting that in the other two parables earlier in this chapter the shepherd left the flock to go and look for the lost sheep and the woman looked for the lost coin by sweeping the floor. Given the two earlier parables we might think that Jesus would have told us that the father left his home and launched a search-and-rescue mission for his son.

But the father waited. At that point in their relationship, reconciliation was only possible if his son *"came to his senses"* (vs. 17). Out of his love, the father respected his son's choice—the only way for the father-son relationship to be restored was for the son to request forgiveness.

The father did not force the issue. He did not hire bounty hunters to kidnap his son and bring him home. The fact that the father did not force the issue did not mean that he had stopped loving his son. I always picture the father sitting on the front porch, gazing wistfully down a long country road, hoping to someday see the distant figure of his son and his familiar gait.

The parable doesn't give us that detail, but it does say that once the father recognized his son he did not wait for him to run the gauntlet of derision and shame as he passed by neighbors on his way home. The father did not require his son to crawl on his knees and kiss his feet, but instead, the father cast all decorum aside, and he ran to meet his barefoot son dressed in rags. Again, we are filled with a picture of the father's unbounded love—*unreserved and undeserved.*

The father's love calls for a lavish celebration with friends, family and neighbors, for that which was lost has been found.

Attention! Attention! Religious authorities please note.

The father does not insist on a public ceremony in which the son gives his "testimony"—with enough lurid details to satisfy the appetite of those who needed their "pound of flesh." The father is not interested in having his son endure some public spectacle so that the father's honor and "good name" can be restored.

Lavish Love and Extravagant Grace

This parable is the polar opposite from so many religious expectations and requirements called for when someone who has "fallen away" wishes to be "restored to the fold." There is no witch hunt, trial or hanging in this parable. There is no gauntlet of scorn, abuse and condemnation the young man needs to endure. There is no contract that the young son is forced to sign promising that he will never again be so stupid and silly.

Nor does the parable say anything about an employment covenant or work-for-hire contract the father draws up, detailing how long the son must work before the inheritance can be paid in full. The lavish love of the prodigal father simply sweeps it all away.

The son is forgiven, and there is no debt to be paid. Once again, the original audience is back on its heels. Once again Jesus deals a major blow to one of the pillars of religion. No restitution? No pay back? No penance? No public confession?

The father and his younger son are equally extravagant, each in their own way, at the other end of the spectrum. The younger son has been unbelievably immature, foolhardy, reckless and irresponsible. He is, beyond any doubt, exhibit "A" for the word *prodigal*.

But wait! The father is also prodigal. He seems to be generous to a fault. When the father's lavish and liberal (wasteful?) use of his resources is carefully considered, it's hard not to think of him as soft headed and soft hearted.

He doesn't seem to care what others think of him—he doesn't seem to worry about his friends or family thinking that his love is so blind that he is allowing his younger son to take advantage of him—again.

What seems, to the human mind, to be lavish wastefulness continues, as the father calls for the best robe in the family to be brought to clothe his son. The best robe would be the father's own robe. The best robe would be a sign of honor and esteem. The father directs that a ring be placed on the son's finger—another sign of full acceptance—and the fattened calf to be killed so that a major celebration could begin.

Religion does not normally encourage its followers to think of God as being in the middle of a big party. We hear of a God of wrath and justice, but do we hear much about God throwing his head back and laughing?

When the father's lavish and liberal (wasteful?) use of his resources is carefully considered, it's hard not to think of him as soft headed and soft hearted.

How often is God depicted as being at the head of a banquet table, drinking and eating way into the night? Just at the time when the laughter and joy reach their crescendo at the party, Jesus introduces religion, in the person of the older brother. Of course, true to form, Christ-less religion is frowning, unhappy that other people seem to be enjoying themselves.

The older brother arrives to complain about the excessive noise and celebration. Perhaps the party was keeping him from his prayers! Jesus doesn't provide all the details of what the perfect, or near-perfect older brother said when he arrived at the party, but we do know he was not a happy camper.

Jesus could have ended the parable at this point, with the celebration, with a warm and fuzzy "and they lived happily ever after." But Jesus concludes the parable by addressing condemnation, the all-too-common religious reaction to God's grace.

The older brother was miffed at the extravagant, over-the-top celebration of the father's endless love. He felt scandalized that he had not been recognized for all his years of what he characterized as slaving for his father (vs. 29).

The younger brother felt that he was no longer worthy to be his father's son. In his mind, the relationship he once enjoyed was gone forever. The best relationship with his father he could ever hope for would be as a hired servant (vs. 19). By contrast, the older brother was still "at home." All physical indicators pointed toward a positive relationship with his father. But while the older brother obeyed his father, he begrudgingly obeyed. He felt he earned a positive relationship with his father on the basis of "slaving" for him—never disobeying him (vs. 29). The older brother felt that he deserved his father's love and that his younger brother did not.

WE SEARCH IN VAIN IN THIS PARABLE FOR ANY HINT OF THE ANGRY God THAT CHRIST-LESS RELIGION DEPICTS. THERE IS NO HINT OF A SINNER IN THE HANDS OF AN ANGRY God.

The older brother was absolutely appalled that a party was being thrown for his younger brother, the scoundrel that he was, while no party had ever been thrown for him, the good, rule-keeping son. The older brother felt justified in refusing to attend the party, and thus, by his public boycott, perhaps humiliate his father, for everyone would be asking about his glaring absence.

The older brother felt that his younger brother had offended their father in the first place, so why couldn't he? Of course, the older brother was now aware that his no-good brother had not only been forgiven, without any need to make restitution, but restored to a full place of honor in the family.

If you've ever heard about or personally experienced a family doing the numbers about who receives what regarding an inheritance, and the often fiery debates that follow, you'll have an idea of what the older brother must have been thinking.

First of all, the younger brother got his inheritance when he left home. For the purpose of discussion, let's just round off the estimated value of the family farm at a million dollars.

There's no need to discuss all of the inheritance laws and procedures in place at that time, because clearly the father's extravagant, prodigal love had already set them aside. Let's presume that when the younger son asked for his share of the family farm the father decided to give him a one-third share ($333,333.33). The remaining $666,666.66 (I hope all those sixes don't freak out any of my prophecy-minded readers) would, of course, be retained by the father.

Let's assume the father may have made out his will at that time, leaving his older son with a one-third share, equal to that of his younger brother, while stipulating that the father's own one-third share would be divided, upon his death, by his two sons.

Of course, the early part of the parable makes it clear that neither the younger son, the father, nor the older brother expected the younger son to ever come back home. You don't have to get out your pencil to understand at least one reason why the older brother was not too excited to see his younger brother back home again. His younger brother's return was costing him money!

The older son was furious at what he interpreted as an obvious miscarriage of justice. His father seemed far more concerned about love and forgiveness and grace than he did justice. That fear is the very fear that institutionalized religion has of the grace of God.

The father, who had left the house to greet his returning younger son, now did the same for his older son. The father's love was the same for both sons. The father had no favorites. The father, once he realized that his older son was offended and self-righteously indignant, left the house to go and reason and plead with his older son.

But the older son would have none of his father's explanations. The older son publicly castigated his father, implying that his father had not treated him fairly and that his father had not rewarded him in a manner that was commensurate with his work. The older brother felt his father was unfair. "All" he wanted was justice (as he perceived it).

The older brother attempted to distance himself from his younger brother by telling his father that the younger brother was this "son of yours" (vs. 30), obviously implying that he was no brother of his.

Churches in the Hands of an Angry God?

His father continued to reach out to the older brother. We search in vain in this parable for any hint of the angry God that Christ-less religion depicts. There is no hint of a sinner in the hands of an angry God. There is no teaching that would have us think that the father is a God of wrath, whose wrath must be placated so that what grace-less religion interprets as justice may be done.

Similar to the emphasis you will hear within many denominations and churches today, the older brother wanted justice. He wanted to see his younger brother "get what's coming to him"—but his father was not interested in seeing the younger son get what he deserved.

The father's love was *unreserved* and *undeserved*. The father told the older brother that he still had a brother, and that he ought to be happy because *"this brother of yours was dead and is alive again; he was lost and is found"* (vs. 32).

HERE IS AN INCREDIBLE PORTRAIT OF GOD'S INFINITE LOVE. IT'S A PICTURE OF THE RELATIONSHIP GOD OFFERS TO EVERYONE, TO EACH ONE OF US, NO MATTER WHO WE ARE OR WHAT WE HAVE DONE.

Realizing that his father would not give his younger brother what he deserved, the older son then demanded what he felt he deserved—and the father told the older son that *"everything I have is yours"* (vs. 31).

The parable ends with the door to the father's house wide open to his older son. The younger son had left his father's house by his own choice, and, upon deciding to come home, had entered his father's house, by grace. The door was wide open. No conditions. No penance. No humiliation.

The older son was scandalized by God's grace, and the parable ends without us knowing whether he entered that open door, "gracing" the party with his presence. The older son believed that his father's love should be solely reserved for him because he deserved it. But he completely misunderstood his father's love. The love of our Father in heaven is *unreserved and undeserved.*

Here is an incredible portrait of God's infinite love. It's a picture of the relationship God offers to everyone, to each one of us, no matter who we are or what we have done.

This parable is also a picture of the condemnation we humans heap on others whom we feel to be less deserving than we are. The parable ends without a response from the older, rules-keeping-and-proud-of-it brother.

For that matter, many institutionalized churches refuse to let the parable end as Jesus did. Jesus left the outcome uncertain. But legalistic religion just can't let the parable end that way. People might just take the "grace thing" too far.

Following the first-century, as the church became an institution, it determined that it couldn't allow just anyone to join or remain a member. It needed standards—doctrines—dogmas—creeds. As the institutionalized church adopted systems and methodologies to control those it "served," it encountered God's grace—liberally sprinkled throughout the New Testament.

The most effective way to deal with God's grace would have been to declare all passages which taught or hinted at grace as undeserving of a place in the biblical canon. But that option was way too obvious.

Christ-less religion came up with another alternative. It responded to grace with protocols, practices and policies which were taught as the basis and foundation of faith.

These procedures then became accepted as benchmarks of right belief. They determined the way in which biblical statements would be interpreted. Here are but a few of many examples that occur to me:

> By placing its own doctrines and dogmas before God's grace and before the Son, Christ-less religion effectively reinterpreted many teachings to fit its own needs.

• Since God only loves Christians (members of our club), even though John 3:16 says he loves the whole world, the Bible actually doesn't mean what it seems to say.

• Since God would never want all his laws of the Old Testament to be irrelevant, replaced by grace, when the New Testament talks about grace it actually doesn't mean what it might seem to.

• Since God is a no-nonsense God of wrath and justice, the parable of the prodigal son can't actually mean what it seems to say.

In terms of the teaching of the parable of the lost sons, religion effectively edited the parable with its own values and culture—so that its spin on Jesus' teaching held sway in the hearts and minds of its followers.

Christ-less religion marinated teachings like the parable of the prodigal/lost son in its own stew of doctrines and dogmas, so that when the religious cooks were finished with it, this parable, along with many other passages, was stripped of the radical grace of Jesus Christ.

By placing its own doctrines and dogmas before God's grace and before the Son, Christ-less religion effectively reinterpreted many teachings to fit its own needs.

One of the most sinister teachings of all concerns the cross of Christ. Christ-less religion eventually interpreted the cross in such a way as to give prominence to its rules and regulations. The teaching came to be known as *penal substitution*— Jesus took our place, receiving the penalty we would otherwise receive from the father.

The penal substitution teaching insists that the cross was all about (and still is, at many religious addresses) the wrath of the Father being poured out, because, according to religion, our sins had offended his honor and holiness. In order to restore the Father's honor the Son was killed in an honor-killing.

This is but one of many dogmas that religion established as "truth" which, once accepted, cast doubts on the degree of God's love and grace.

As a further example, let's actually re-write the parable of the prodigal/lost son in the way that many slaves of religion today actually understand it.

I am indebted for the germ of this idea to Robin Collins of Messiah College in Pennsylvania, and his 1995 paper, "Understanding Atonement: A New and Orthodox Theory."

Here's an abbreviated idea of what a literal re-write of the parable of the lost sons, inspired by the doctrines and dogmas of Christ-less religion, might look like:

The youngest of two sons asked his father for his share of the family farm. When he received his share, the youngest son left home and squandered his inheritance, walking on the wild side in a far away land. When he had run out of money, he came back home, desperate and destitute.

When he asked his father to forgive him and just give him a job, like a hired hand, the father said, "I can't just forgive you. You've insulted my honor. I can't trivialize sin. Restitution will have to be made. There's a debt to be paid. My wrath will have to be satisfied."

The good son, the elder son, heard about how upset his father was, so he came to his father and said, "Why don't you let me pay the debt my brother owes? I will work extra hard to satisfy your honor so that your wrath can be appeased and pacified."

So the older brother took the place of his younger brother, working so long and so hard that finally he collapsed from exhaustion. When the older brother died, the father then told his youngest son that he had been forgiven. From then on the younger son was careful not to upset his father and they lived happily ever after.

AFTERWORD

TWO CAPTAINS

I n Steven Spielberg's movie *Saving Private Ryan*, a squadron of soldiers in the European theatre of World War II is sent on a mission to find one soldier behind enemy lines and bring him home. Many of the young men, including the Captain, die *Saving Private Ryan*. A grateful Private Ryan kneels over the dying Captain who led the successful rescue effort. With the tremendous sacrifices of life necessary to ensure Private Ryan's safety in mind, the dying Captain's last words to Private Ryan are "earn this."

Saving Private Ryan fast forwards from the young Private Ryan in World War II to senior citizen Private Ryan. In a pilgrimage back to the battlefields and military cemeteries of Europe Private Ryan is accompanied by his wife, grown children and grandchildren as he pays his respects. He visits the grave of his Captain, who decades earlier had instructed him to "earn" the sacrifices that were made to save his life.

Private Ryan kneels at the grave and says, to the deceased Captain, "Not a day goes by I don't think about what happened...and I just want you to know...I've tried. Tried to live my life the best I could. I hope that's enough. I didn't ever invent anything. I didn't cure any diseases. I worked on a farm. I raised a family. I lived a life. I only hope, in your eyes at least, I earned what you did for me."

We all feel somewhat like Private Ryan in that we live our lives trying to "earn" something. Of course, there's nothing spiritually problematic about wanting to please our parents, make our spouses proud, provide for our family and leave something behind for our children. But much of the emphasis on working hard to earn the plaudits and admiration of others seeps into our relationship with God.

> **MUCH OF THE EMPHASIS ON WORKING HARD TO EARN THE PLAUDITS AND ADMIRATION OF OTHERS SEEPS INTO OUR RELATIONSHIP WITH God.**

Our 21st-century North American culture evaluates a life "lived well" in terms of successful attempts to earn, build and accumulate treasures. A life "lived well" is felt to be exemplified by items displayed in a trophy case—diplomas and certificates—as well as treasures hidden in safe deposit boxes and bank accounts—deeds of trust, bank notes and retirement accounts. But it's a huge mistake to approach our relationship with God in a similar way.

"What good will it be for someone to gain the whole world, yet forfeit their soul?" (Matthew 16:26).

The kingdom of heaven operates on the principle and currency of grace. We are invited to receive God's grace and accept, without stipulation or reservation, what Jesus has done for us.

He is truly the *"Captain of our salvation"* (Hebrews 2:10, King James Version).

He does not ask us to do the impossible—for it is truly impossible for us to earn his love and grace. He doesn't ask us to prove our worthiness for the grace so freely given to us. He did not look down from his cross and say "earn this." Our Captain simply invites us to receive the grace of our Lord we can never earn.

—SDG

God's amazing grace is:

- God's unmerited goodness and generosity.
- God's gift to us of his favor (love), approval and acceptance we can never deserve or earn.
- The means/channel/fountainhead through which God delivers his love to humans.
- The unconditional economy of God. God's grace is the way he works and operates, which is the opposite of the oh-so human *you-do-something-for-me-and-I'll-do-something-for-you* economy of the kingdoms of this world. God's grace is given with no strings attached.
- A gift of such magnitude that no repayment is possible, let alone required.
- A gift based on God's goodness, whch is the foundation of his relationship with us, rather than the religious relationship we are so often told we can earn on the strength of our deeds.
- A spiritual state/environment/condition in which God's children live.
- God's desire and seemingly reckless abandon in relentlessly pursuing his creation with his love.

God's grace is his *in-spite-of* what we have done love, as opposed to the religious idea that God loves us *because of* what we have done. God's grace expresses his desire to love us always, as the father did in the parable of the prodigal son. God's grace means that he will never, ever give up on us.